# Forcible Love
## NTN Version

## by

## orde

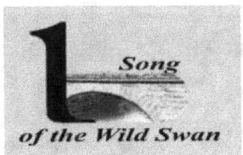

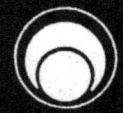

*NTN presents for Independence Festivities*

# Forcible Love

## a musical drama on the life of

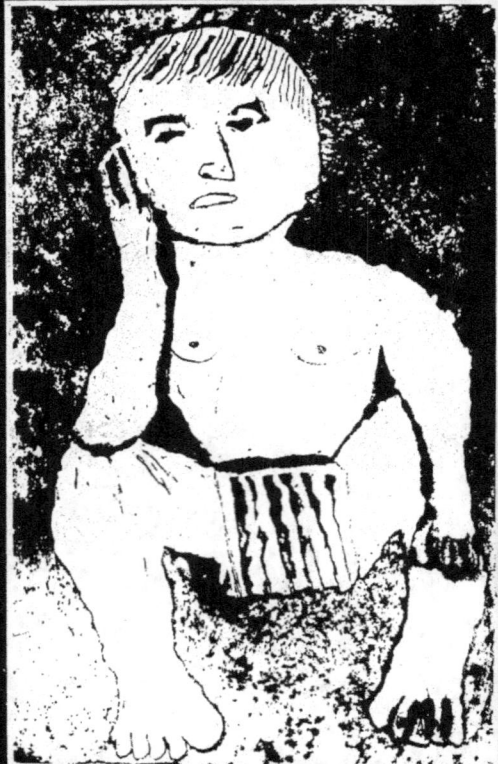

*John*

# Muafangejo

Published by Song, 2014.
Song is an Imprint of:
Song of the Wild Swan Ltd.
1 Folly Bridge, Oxford, OX1 4LB, UK.
www.songwildswan.com
tel +44 (0) 1865 240572
fax +44 (0) 1865 246565
e: info@songwildswan.com

***Forcible Love(NTN Version)*** **by orde**
**ISBN 9781909777187**

First published: 1991 (Private, 30 copies).
eBook: 2014 Song, Oxford.

# Acknowledgements

Song eBook Design series by Laurence Hutton-Smith.
Cover Design: Laurence Hutton-Smith.
Cover Image: Mother and Child 1979, John Muafangejo, linocut, [Lev.134]
Frontispiece: Cover of Programme for National Theatre Production
Independence Festivities, Sad Boy 1985 John Muafangejo, etching, [Lev.226].
Book Production: Amaury Marinho Junior

All illustrations by John Muafangejo by kind permission of the John
Muafangejo Trust, © John Muafangejo Trust, Oxford, 2014.

The author is grateful to the following authors, translators and publishers for
permission to include extracts in this play of:

*The Paradox* by Francesca Yétúndé Pereira © Francesca Pereira

*Lonely* by Bloke Modsisane © Bloke Modsisane

Extracts from an interview (unpublished at the time) between Pedro Vorster
and John Muafangejo © Pedro Vorster/John Muafangejo Trust.

4

# Contents

# Foreword

When I began to review and correct text, spelling and proofs for the eBook and print on demand publications it became apparent that it was to be correcting more than just the spelling and layout. The work had been written in a way that had a flavor of the period and the heady atmosphere of both the independence celebrations at the time; the work of Muafangejo and its discussion amongst new converts; and the adaptation (inserting sections, re-arranging, changing to the NTN version) written in a short space of time and amongst actors who had never acted before, and in a variety of languages. Adaptation was key. Looking at it now, it is hand-carved with this imprint, with sections in bold print, italic print, font size variations, phonetic spellings, apparent mis-spellings (e.g. whichdoctor) and possibly even errors of spelling. In trying to correct this for the eBook/print on demand something important was being lost. Another example is of Ible and Able (Scene Fourteen): I had to debate if fossible was a new variation linking back to the richness of age old time fossils or as simple as 'ss' where an 'rc' should be. Or was I trying to emphasize phonetics. I cannot remember. Perhaps all of them but its richness lay in leaving it as it is.

So too with Scene two – the Efundula ceremony is rich and symbolic and to the cast – many of whom were Kuanjama's – would know it so there was no need to elaborate on it other than the pars pro toto element as I did at the time, and there are references to works that fully explain the ceremony. It is not a bad thing to work under time pressure where meaning is clear and understood by actors who need no instruction in their cultural heritage. It's best to leave it as it was at the time. The only exceptions I made was to give the meaning of the Kuanjama names or phrases that appear, which were not listed in the glossary at the time.

Aside from the above addition to the glossary, I decided not, therefore, to edit and update or correct but to leave the work the way it had been printed. I like it even more so now, as it reminded me of the time and place, and I see now Muafangejo's own way of working – a focus on content and feelings, not on grammar. And the different size text, indentation, spelling has its own character especially with the different languages being used.

Its existing style is also a 'nod' of respect to Picasso, who introduced curtains as a character in his play, and I remember I had the slides in as 'characters' while stagehands were introduced as l and r for left and right. While I hope the content holds its own at all times, the format of it was suitable then, and I feel, still is.

orde

Oxford, 10 April 2014

6

# National Theatre of Namibia (NTN)

Costume Design:        Katja Horchen
                                  Martha Hashikutuva

Costumes:                 Mrs Heath
                                  Martha Hashikutuva
                                  Katja Hornchen
                                  Patricia Vusani

Lighting Design:        Mark Behrens
Set Design:             Bobby Heath, Terence Zeeman
Sound Design:         Mark Behrens, Rita Louise Hofmeyer,
                                  Terence Zeeman

Lighting Operator:     Roy Krotz, Ronald Bosman
Follow Spot:           John Gephardj, Ananias Namalenga
Sound Operator:       Speedy Wolgast
Stage Hands:          Theophilus Wekonga
                                  Benji Jonas
                                  Elias Garoeb
                                  Amoni Rameka

Director:                Terence Zeeman
Artistic Director:     orde

*Special Thanks to:*

Melonie Pretorius
Sandy Rudd
The Ministry of Education and Culture
The John Muafangejo Foundation
Namibian Arts Association
The Heinitzberg Castle Arts Centre
Ian Flemming
Minnette Mans
Prof Behrens
Struppi Reinhart
Jo Roth
University of Namibia
Windhoek Players
Linda Naude

Normally an artist (authors included) sees their creation like a mother sees their new-born child – with a little bit of blind love, but much protection. Any attempt to harm either of these creations, results in massive retaliation and understandably so.

But an artist is not always so insistently protective. If I may misquote Goethe the artist, as a poet, as a man and as a citizen will love his Native Land; but the native land of his artistic powers and artistic action is the good, noble and beautiful which is confined to no particular province or country and which he seizes upon and forms where ever he finds himself.

Workshopping – working in production with others on a creation – is nothing new in theatre but here it was: a play began in my mind some time ago – then more for TV to tie in with the Muafangejo Museum show currently touring UK museums. Aside from the title "Forcible Love" and a 'picture' of the acts and scenes, I never really got round to writing it. Then the curator of the Heinitz Castle Art Centre phoned me to say that during the Muafangejo exhibition there the schoolchildren from the Shipena High School had, on the tour of the castle, been asked by the NTN staff – who were present to talk to them about the show – to improvise a drama on his death. This was so successful that Terence Zeeman mentioned the idea of the play to the curator, Melonie Pretorius, who talked to me about it. About 8 weeks ago when I returned from Oxford, I saw Terence and we began examining the possibility with the cast. I returned to Oxford to write while the cast continued to workshop suggested scenes.

About three weeks before opening I faxed to Terence the 21 draft pages of the first act and we spoke. I was both thrilled and nervous – thrilled with what he mentioned about its direction and enthusiasm of the cast – and nervous not only because I was not getting across my vision of the play – that is the workshopped scenes were not in line with what I had conceived – but also because two weeks were simply not enough time to rehearse. About 20 min after my fax I refaxed saying we should postpone. Then I called to confirm this but Terence re-assured me not to worry that it would work and that it would be impossible to postpone because most of his lead actors were being invited to Denmark. Ironically, what also influenced me in coming out was the way Terence described the enthusiasm of the cast for the production and more specifically that many of the Kuanyamas were inexperienced in conventional theatre – from my experience in art history, sometimes the untrained has a heart that is open – that responds direct from the soul and this is always enriching.

So out I came preparing for the worst – the workshop scenes were excellent, the songs fine and very catchy, the third act impossible to incorporate, the second act had to be re-arranged and number of parts rewritten.

My protective instincts were up. In theory an author's (and a director's) nightmare. Then it struck me – painters have been known to do graphics with only colour variations – to see the different moods. Why not a variation – call it "Forcible Love (NTN version)". I think Terence had come to the same, conclusion. This I think is unique in theatre – for what there might be is two plays by the same author but with "colour variants". We have worked wonderfully. Certainly my "final version" (if this is just a variant) will incorporate most of the workshopped scenes and many ideas have flown from this collaboration. I can only thank the NTN and the cast for the forcible (!) way they have involved themselves in the production – heartfelt thanks must be given to them especially in the song and dance numbers. And of course to the staff at NTN – all who contributed and to Allen Ambor – who 8 days before opening night was faxed the script and was on the plane the" next day, having set aside all his other commitments. Yes I suppose the commitment from all has been gratifying for me and I have learnt much about Kuanyama words and traditions – direct from source – people enacting them. Nuances of the Kuanyama language have fascinated me – also the declensions (I thought of my wasted time at school decling 'amo, amas, amat' – which seems almost as difficult as Kuanyama) and the rich interplay of words.

But there were also other practical reasons for a variation. The Director had to explain to actors who had never acted what is to be done, learning lines, and more this was done via an interpreter as the Kuanyamas could not speak English. And more what also had to be explained is watch out for that trapdoor etc. And more – how do you explain or justify to a Kuanyama that the wedding scene must be condensed – that this is art, a play – to 10 minutes when normally it is a three month ceremony. What a challenge to all – to the director to keep the pace if not the peace – what wonderful information and very moving to an author to incorporate – almost a play in itself – on directing.

But it went even further than the Kuanyamas never having been on stage – I had a scene with a reporter – who to cast? – then I thought why not ask a reporter who knew Muafangejo and had interviewed Muafangejo and on whom I based the scene to play the part. It is a first time for him in the theatre.

Another interesting fact was that there was not a sufficient budget (even to rehearse with the full cast) – I understand that the budget of this production is a record low for the NTN (and for most productions) – it was around R12,000 including sets and designs. But I also learnt that this is relative. At rehearsals was a director from Zamibia who was interested in performing the play there and asked how much it had cost to put on – when I said it cost the NTN around R12,000 he murmured "so much".

9

I think this type of workshopping has been a growth for everyone and it is so because of the absolute trust that was created and meant. To place your new-born baby in someone else's hands is always fraught with anxiety and danger. I think I can say and I think that the entire cast will agree that it is a very healthy child – one that I think will grow into one that can hold its head anywhere. It remains to be seen if there will be the oohs and aahs etc. that one normally bestows on children of the Father Land and Mother Africa.

orde
Windhoek
17 March 1991

## Cast:

Usher/s
The Pictures
Ndevasia Muafangejo
John Muafangejo
John Ndevasia Muafangejo
Petelena Hamupolo
Curator
Opening Speaker/s
Purchaser
Pupils
Teacher
Voice:
University examiners
Border guard
Kuanyamas/Tswanas/Zulus/Namas
Whichdoctor
Whichdoctor's assistant
Bishop
Priest
Pressman
L/R

# Scene One

(A single Kuanyama bowman playing Okambulumbumbua – the gourd part of the instrument must be placed over the heart)

Sings:      Omwiya wange wa Nangolo wahola Ngishi-nande wemuhola nokumu laya. Shimbwidanga ya Ndamona ya Namutenya novana ya Nghishekwa na Malondo la Matondo lambadangela ohatunhu kaNgule na Taitama lohumshito lohDndonga GaMatope, Ndjaba mutwe ya Nangolo yoo Shingwadja shikwiyu ya Mwahafa Hamunime, Okaima kada-lwa ohapofi kadalwa phapamhadali okatwika mesho namwengu kamena tete eumbinga omatwi inaa mbaduka

# Scene Two

Kuanyama Efundula ceremony –

See Notes:

the final stage towards marriage

the first day - men beat drums as the girls enter, with a dancing want

the second day - okambadyona receiving of the mug of beer (omupitifi) from a man which he spills over them girls who crawl through his legs. Know the girls are known as ovafuko

the third day - (ombadje yakula) is when the girls show their strength in dancing

the fourth day - (omuhlo) girls wear decoration and dancing and symbolic engagements are made – Ongoleka (friend of male lover) ties a strip of palm leaf across his shoulder and under the shoulder of the bride. If she breaks it there is no marriage – if she does not there is a marriage

note Ometela headress in Muafangejo works – signifies a bull and cow – front two the cow and the back three the bull – with the headdress the girls should wear the ash clothes.

# Scene Three/Four: at the border

Symbolic division of Kuanyama tribe into the area of Angola and Namibia –

When the Kuanyama have departed two are left playing – the guard enters and they do not notice the guard who comes up to them when their hands are linked and then breaks the linkage suddenly – they flee to separate sides of the stage with him standing at the point – his right hand is stretched down with finger pointing at the ground and he slowly raises it – keeping it stiff – through the arc of pointing at the audience, the Hitler salute and until it points to Heaven. He/she holds it pointing upwards – slowly withdraws the pointed finger into a clenched fist and drops it very suddenly. Walks up and down a few times along the imaginary boundary and thus makes it real.

B/Guard: (moves to one side of the now real border that he has created and says in Afrikaans accent) Angola (then moves to the other side of the border line and says in German accent) SudwesAfrika (then returns to a position where he can straddle the border)

Voice: I stand on the border between two countries. An artificial boundary that divides the Kuanyama people... straight down the middle. (pause points to one side and says in English)..... Angola, (points to the other side and says) South West Africa (goes to the guard from the Angolan side – hands his imaginary travel/identity papers)

Border: And who are you?

Voices: A voice

Border-guard: (very gruffly) What

Voice: (pause) I am the narrator

B. G.: Oh (examines papers – lets him through to the Namibian side)

Voice: Oh, I almost forgot to introduce myself. I am the Voice – a sort of story teller if you like. Many stories are told by many people – some we only remember vaguely – some we never forget – some are written – some are true stories – some are more true than others – these are told in pictures – word pictures, written pictures, music pictures whatever – we all have different ways of communicating – I am the kind that is here but not here – perhaps the onlooker – no different to you out there (gestures to the audience) except perhaps a little more privileged because I am part of the story. I will fill in the gaps between the stories and dances and songs of this strange tale. For instance, John's mother will soon be crossing the border. She'll become an Anglican. Anglican Kuanyamas must dress in an Anglican way. So, she'll need a dress – an Anglican dress.

(Petelena Hamupolo enters in traditional Kuanyama clothes)

Here she comes now.

PH crosses to border – hands imaginary papers and as these are being examined slowly removes some of her garments – placing them in a bundle on her head (if this is impossible to do then the bundle must be clutched to her heart). The guard silently examines her and lets her through to the Namibian side where the Voice comes up to her.

V:             There is a work (Slide of She is divorcing 1969 [Lev.161]) of John's called she is divorcing her husband with her children" ... I wonder – an artist remembering many years later what it felt like to be abandoned by a mother who just disappeared when his father died – took on the white man's god? Who imagined what it is like for a mother to divorce herself with her children and leave.

(Voice materialises and walks up to Petelena who is standing on the Namibian side of the border) She'll be taking communion soon. Soon, she will have another name – for Kuanyama names are heathen and pagan....and a bit difficult to pronounce. So her name will probably change to Ruth or Esther of the Bible. She must change her gods, her dress, (helps her with a dress which he has taken out – a simple elegant white smock but which is in the shape of a straight jacket so that she can enter her arms and have it tied behind her back) in fact, change everything about her (the voice then takes a cross which he puts on her – if the bundle is on her head she must lift it and tilt her head to accept the cross around her neck – if it is clasped to her, the voice must put it on her via the 'neck' of the bundle – the symbolism must be clear.

The 'Bible says, "If any man is in Christ, you become a new creature," (she moves on and takes a corn stamper and begins to corn stamp, happily (see They are stamping the corn, c1970 [Lev.36] for imagery of a corn stamper)

But John, that's his Anglican name, has yet to become a Christian. (Ndevsia Muafangejo enters in traditional kraal outfit with bow and arrow (see work). He's twelve years old now, and has walked two days to the Border. That's the lad now....

(NM goes to border guard – they say nothing and he is allowed to cross. He reaches his mother who stops stamping and clasps him to her heart and Patelena Hampulo and Ndevsia Muafangejo talk to each other in Kuanyama

See, (image of They are shaking their hands 1981 [Lev.179]) they are shaking their hands because they are longing for each other,"

They are speaking Kuanyama on the Anglican South West side of the border. Let me translate:

| | |
|---|---|
| PH | Ndevasia omati yange owakula |
| Voice | Ndevisia, my son, you have grown |
| NM | Meme oshike wa tauluk eengamba wetufiyapo |
| Voice | My mother, why have you crossed the border away from your family. |
| PH | Ne delonga. Ome ondeye oku opo ndininge omukriste<br>I have come to find God – the father |
| NM | Meme oshikik wandjala oikuto eyi hayo wali hondjala nale |
| Voice | Mother, why do you wear such strange clothes. |
| PH | Ame paife omukriste omati. wange ei oyo oikuto yokeiya nayo kongerti |
| Voice | I am a Christian now...so I wear the clothes of the church. |
| NM | Oshi shili [oshikesh] |
| Voice | and what is that around your neck |
| PH | mofino yoye |

14

| | |
|---|---|
| Voice | It is the cross of Christ |
| NM | owu omushiyakano wengerki oterushu – omushiyakan |
| Voice | If I want to be the cross of Christ what shall I do mother |
| PH | Ohandi fikama Ndikutwale ko Ngeleka kamwange |
| Voice | Let me take you to the father. He can explain the creation. (Slide of Adam and Eva 1968 [Lev.1] by Muafangejo) (They move holding hands to kneeling position as the bishop in full and imposing regalia enters to the sound of Verdi's requiem – Kuanyama drums are heard – and singing – Ndevesia flees the stage in terror – (the guard meanwhile has slowly exited on the other side to Ndevesia's) the cast and John enter, John goes to kneel alongside his mother who then leaves by the same exit as the guard – the cast acts as chorus – some are in Anglican dress (same simple dress with cross as Petulena has) some in Kuanyama dress – the border guard re-enters from the opposite side that he exited – ie where NM exited – moves around them touching/striking, at the instruction of the Bishop, those that in Kwanyama dress, who fall screaming – the music continues throughout the following dialogues of the Chorus the bishop, (God's) voice and voice. |
| God's voice: | The cross, the icon, the disciples fought They are still fighting |
| Chorus | The whiteman claims His God Supreme and blackman muses (Slides of The Baptised of Christ 1968 [Lev.9]; the Bishop 1969 [Lev.28], which changes to Confirmation 1980 [Lev.162]) |
| God's voice: | In the beginning was the Word, and the Word was with God and the Word was God |
| Voice: | Whose God? Kuanyama God, Anglican God, Christian God, Hebrew God, Muslim God. Whose God? |
| Bishop: | The Word was God |

| | |
|---|---|
| Chorus | The disciples fought. They all of them join battle (John turns to face the audience and begins beating an imaginary drum) |
| Male voices: | fierce raging – each god is mighty (the border guard (who has now knocked down all Kuanyamas) goes and stands behind JM who is still beating the imaginary drum and is facing the audience) .. and watches |
| Voice: | They must be. It must be. The world is constant in its chaos. |
| Chorus: | The world is crumbling and all gods are silent. |
| Female voices: | Evil begets evil. Good begets evil. Watching. Wenching eves, empty headed apes. |
| Chorus | Demanding, exacting. |
| God's voice: | And the Infant crying for the dried-up stream. |
| Chorus: | The drum still beats on – the fevered drum – still blind – beats wildly – fiercely – forcefully on |

(Music – the guard touches points to those of the Kuanyamas that are down and they rise putting on white gowns with crosses like Petulena (moving around with their hands in the prayer position)

The bishop moves to centre stage where four of the Kuanyamas who were down and are now 'converted' kneel in front of him – they have their back to the audience and Muafangejo must be between them and the audience – he has stopped beating the imaginary drum and is on his knees but raised his arms and spread them out into the crucifixion position – the bishop faces the four kneeling Kuanyamas (who have taken the border guards position of being behind John – the guard having exited) – chorus exits – Music stops – only the bishop, John and four Kuanyamas on stage.

| | |
|---|---|
| B | what is your name |
| Kuanyama | my name, my name is Emanguluko |
| B | Yes well that is too difficult – we shall call you Norman, (turning to Kuanyama) And what is your name |
| K | Mwalengokanja |

16

| | |
|---|---|
| B | Mal what |
| K | Mwalengokanja |
| K | I shall call you Marcha |
| B | And what is your name |
| K | Tukondjeni |
| B | Well since it is St Patricks day I shall call you Patrick. (turning to Kuanyama) whats your name |
| K | Hafeni |
| B | Well since you are next to Patrick I shall call you Patricia (moves to leave) |
| K | Pat-del-icia |
| B | (Amused and irritated) Patricia (begins to move off) |
| K | (nudging Emanguluko – softly) Patri, ah |
| B | Yes well god bless you – go in peace (exits) |

Kuanyamas all exit hands clasped in prayer (blackout for next scene)

## Scene Five: John rebirth and renaming

| | |
|---|---|
| Ndevasia: | (Singing and carving a cup and laughing) |

(a kindly father enters)

| | |
|---|---|
| Father: | (enters and sees John working) Ah John |
| Ndevasia: | Father, father my name is Ndevasia. |
| F | Your name is John (pause) |
| N | Say it. Say my name (pause) Say Ndevasia |

Father:     When you are – when you have been accepted into the Church, and when you become a Christian you become a new person, you are reborn, so therefore your name must change....

Ndevasia:   Father I have my own name (pause) Do you know father, my father, has given me Ndevasia and this name – and he has accepted it – Ndevasia

F           What does it mean

N           Ndevasia – is – koshiva – koshivongo to this name its ah – well I don't know why my father has given me this name – this is something concerned with my father and my father died when my mother still alive

Father:     Yes but your name is just a name that has nothing to do with your new life now – your mother's name Petelena is now Mary

N           The name – the meaning of the name is to invite me to do something – that to, to ask me to be that thing to to be

F           to appoint to

N           to num

F           nominate

N           nom yes is nomi – nated – yes

F           to be nominated

N           so this is the meaning of my name. this thing is good for me – is nice for me. I like it. So before I was born this thing happened already it is where my name has developed and I search for this and I search for it – just last – but my father is dead and I ask I ask my mother one day and she start laughing – first she start laughing – why are you asking your name – I say it is important I have to know what is the meaning of my name – what are you laughing mother – oh it is – she says no I will tell you – it is a secret – so that is a secret between my father and my mother – she say no my father want want something from my mother about the social life and something happened and it was a mistake so

18

my father said I have nominated you (pause) that thing had become a reality so when the baby came so my father give the name.

F      Yes Ja (looks at the cup). But you see John is a bible name and John was a friend of Jesus the Lord – our creator, the Lord asked Jesus to look after his mother – John the disciple was a young man – he wrote the Revelations – he was the one instructed in Love – he was the one who said one can only approach God via love – you have love – you came to Odibo to look for your mother –

N      you can even ask my mother about the names – she know better than me

F      you came to Odibo to look for your mother that is why your name is John because your mother came here to Odibo and she became a Christian and she accepted the new name and you came to Odibo and Jesus nominated John to look after his mother

N      John (pause) but my mother

(general embarrassed pause)

F      Do you like carving?

N      Yes – because I I like to work every day - because I don't have any work to do – its only to do this work – this is the work I like – and I love it.

F      Its ah its ah the time to start thinking about your future – what to do with your life. Would you like to have a position, to stand in the service of the church

N      No. I don't think I am ready to do that – uhm

F      What about the teaching profession

N      What can I teach father

F      John – you can teach many things – you have much inside you – much to teach – when I look at this cup – you can carve – you can teach carving – I see you have put much love in it – look – we can take this and build up – around it

|   |   |
|---|---|
|   | – enlarge it – you can carve – even make sculptures out of wood --we can make so much more of... |
| N | What do you mean father |
| F | But before that you must be taught yourself – Now there is a good Art School at Rorke's Drift in South Africa |
| N | In South Africa? No. |
| F | It is a good school – they will take you there from us – it is an Evangelical Lutheran church school – they have an art and craft centre – they will show you – you will be looked after well – we can ask them to take you |
| N | But South Africa |
| F | There are also good people in South Africa |
| N | I can learn |
| F | Yes |
| N | I can learn carving |
| F | Yes |
| N | Can I even make bigger cups |
| F | Yes (joyously sensing John's participation in his vision and rising in tempo) Big cups – carving on cups – your name on cups – your father on cups – your family on cups – art – you can learn weaving – also pottery |
| N | Then I will go (excitedly walks away – to get ready to go) |
| F | John (Ndevasia does not hear – keeps on walking). Tate |
| N | (turning) father |
| F | What name shall I put down on your application |
| N | (Pauses, examines the cup, tosses it to the father saying) My name is John (the cup is caught by the father). Anglican Artist (as John exits the priest leaves by the other |

direction and passes the voice on the way (who enters – they sort of look at each other kindly)

Voice:      Strange, isn't it – a man becomes an artist by giving up himself – giving up his name – his tribal gods. So what is it that makes up the artist – what makes the artist – not knowing who he is? A desperate search for identity – the desperate search to know.- to teach.... to learn – or is it a loss of known relevancies so that he can discover new paradigms afresh – cross new boundaries – create new worlds, (pause) Rorke's Drift was not as wonderful as the father had imagined.

## Scene Six: Arrival at Rorkes Driff - what is art

A typical pre-class scene they are beginning to assemble – some are playing imaginary headball, others lounging, smoking – and gradually group in front of a very rudimentary chair and table – set to the side of the stage – they chat amongst each other – John enters with tie – they are all very casually dressed – they don't notice him (image of Van Gogh's the potato eaters flashes on screen) they notice John and cease talking – silence as the class sizes up the new pupil – they ignore him and continue talking – the teacher enters unnoticed by all – surveys the class (if the teacher is a woman they must still use the words Sir – which is a to be reverentially used) The teacher very kindly thinks the best way to interrupt them is to begin laughing

T       (Laughing) – good morning class
C       Springing to attention) Good morning Sir
T       (continues laughing at their formality and reverence)
C       (caught slightly off balance – unsure if the teacher is laughing at them or wants to laugh with them – from looking at him they decide with him and laugh)

T       make yourselves at home – sit down

C       (class all sit – John is on the outside of the group, teacher touches/sits on table - not on chair) – Welcome to Rorke's Drift. Many of you may have heard of Rorke's Drift – the big battle. Here we welcome you to the art school. My name is Otto. I am your art teacher. Now who are you?

Class:      (introduce themselves as one with all sorts of names and as they finish we hear John saying very separately from them 'John'

| | |
|---|---|
| T | (unable to cope with all the names but does not want to cause any upsetting of the atmosphere of gentleness and kindness) Glad to meet you all. Sit down |
| C | (sits) |
| T | We are here to learn how to do art – but what is art – Everyone has his own idea about art. Can you tell me what you imagine art is. |
| P1 | Beauty |
| P2 | Crying |
| P3 | Celebration |
| P4 | Fire |
| T | Good. Now I want to tell you about a man called (sees John Muafangejo and touches his head kindly and gently – sensing his outsiderness) What is your name? |
| JM | Ndevasia |
| T | never what |
| JM | John, John Muafangejo |
| T | Pleased to meet you John – now where was I |
| PX | About a man named |
| T | Oh yes – I wanted to tell you about a man called Salvador Dali |
| P | Silver dollars |
| P to girl: | (correcting the word dollars and snuggling up to the girl) daaarling |
| T | (laughing) Not silver dollars, darlings - Salvador Dali – a |

great Spanish painter[1] – Now Salvadore Dali was invited to give a lecture about art in a big hall – much bigger than this one – and he arrived at the hall in some big limosines and (slight pause) a couple of trucks – and the trucks were filled with (shapes a round object with his hands)

PX          Soccer balls

T           No (shapes a round object with his hands)

PZ          Rugby balls

T           (Laughing but louder) No! (shapes a round object with his hands)

PY          Cricket balls

T           (still amused but more louder still) NO! (pause) water melons

Class       water melons

T           Yes. Water melons. And you know what Salvadore Dali did with them – he took the water-melons (shapes a round object with his hands) – took out a knife (Takes an imaginary knife out – echoes of the same gestures as the guard dividing the Kuanyamas) and cut one of them into two, he held up half a water melon to his audience and said (pause) this is Art

P           Ag man that is stupid

T           Well it just goes to show that there are many ideas of art. (moving) and there are many ways of expressing those ideas, (pause and moving amongst the class who have to turn and watch him) Now tell me about the – the different art forms – In what ways do we express art?

P1          Dancing

P2          Singing

---

[1]         The teacher must not use the word artist by mistake

| | |
|---|---|
| P3 | Painting |
| P4 | woodcutting |
| P5 | (jokingly) cutting water melons (seriously) sir |
| C and T | laughs |
| T | (approaches P5 in a joking/menacing way, class falls silent, |
| P5 | backs off pointing to Dali story half joking/half trying to cover his joke if the consequences were serious for him) – |
| PX | (to the rescue) sculpture |
| T | (turning to PX) sculpture (turning to P5 with ideas formulating – class laughs) sculpture – lets make a sculpture out of you (drags him to the table as the class laugh, whistle and interject) |
| P | cut him in half |
| T | (stands P5 on top of the table and contemplates him then begins to adjust his hands, face, body and legs humming/singing to himself as he does so – in particular the hand must be adjusted so that the fingers are reaching out almost touching – any picture can do eg Michaelangelo's hands, Adam and Eve etc and the head must be turned away from the class – pauses to examine his 'artwork' – turns to class and walks away from the 'sculpture' – P5 as he is talking the sculpture P5 slowly turns his head to see what is happening) If I had a knife and a piece of wood I would have carved him (turns back to 'sculpture' and sees that the head is turned – pauses – then goes back to the sculpture and turns the head to the original position) out of wood, (turns to class and walks away from the 'sculpture' – P5, the sculpture turns his head to see what the teacher is doing) then we would have a wooden sculpture – If bronze I would have cast |

(turns back to "sculpture" and sees that the head is turned
– pauses – then goes back to the sculpture and turns the
head to the original position)
him in metal,
(turns to class and walks away form the 'sculpture' – P5,
the sculpture turns his head to see what the teacher is
doing),
if our sculpture were made of
(turns back to 'sculpture' and sees that the head is turned –
-goes back to the sculpture – eye contact – smiles and
throws the sculpture in a forward flip over his back – the
point being made that it is not a sculpture and some 'sport'
is required – turns to class)
all right all of you lets use our imagination and make some
sculptures –
(points to various groups)
you two and you and you
(the class begin to sculpt each other – some just form
joint/triple sculptures – the teacher gets on shoulder of one
student to command anyone who has not paired/trippled
up and is whirled around the 'gallery')

T        put me down (nervously) put me down
(John has not paired up, nor has one Girl, PG, who will be
the girl who talks to him later to make friends and dances
with him, John is busy looking at all the sculptures the girl
is just standing, the teacher notices this – thinks – calls
John) John let sculpt you
(beckons to John and the girl and sculpts them in a forced
position – bending them, then making them face each
other then pinching their cheeks to a forced kiss position)

T        This sculpture I shall call Forcible Love (turning to all the
sculptures) think of names for all your work – hold your
positions – remain just like that – dont move I shall be
right back (exits) (the class realise that the teacher is
playing a game with them – about imagination and reality
and that he is not coming back)

P        Eeh – the teacher is not coming back -(moves) lets dance

C        (all) yes lets dance, lets dance (the imagery is one from
frozen sculptures to vivid dancing – art forms and they
break the frozen positions straight into the dance)

| | |
|---|---|
| C | Yeah (begin clapping, which glides into a rhythmic clapping) |
| | (in the dance sequence and songs and subsequent isolation of John the theme is communication problems and that john wants to work work work – Simultaneously with John moving away to the table where he sits down and begins to work on an imaginary lino, carving – the rest of the cast begin the song – the orchestration is jazz – the females sing Forcible Love the males the refrain) |

## Scene Seven: The Forcible Love Song and snake dance

| | |
|---|---|
| C-F | Forcible Love |
| C-M | Bum bum bum bum bam bam bam |
| C-F | (with whistling) Forcible Love |
| C-M | (with whistling) Bam bam bam bam |
| C-F | Forcible Love |
| C-M | Bam bam bam bam |
| C-F | Forcible Love |
| C-M | Bum bum bum bum bam bam bam |

(P1, an earthy girl detaches herself from the singing snake dance, having noticed that John is alone and goes up to him, very friendly – as she detaches the rest gesticulate with their hands and cat call her, whistling and sniggering – sound changes to earthy guteral sound)

| | |
|---|---|
| P1 | Sa-ukubona buti. Kunjani |
| JM | I dont understand Zula |
| P1 | Uphumaphi wena. Mina ngiphuma kwa Zulu or Durban. Woza siye e Patini. |
| JM | I'm busy |
| P1 | Uyazi yini. Forcible Love. |

26

(more group dancing – approaching John and the girl PG – who was sculpted in forcible love with him, approaches)

PG      Hey! John. What are you doing.

JM      I am busy working

PG      Which work. Come and join the party. We are busy dancing. Put this away (pushes his imaginary tools aside) put this away. Come on get up get up (drags him to his feet) John get up (all this with many whistles and catcalls – they dance John awkwardly at first then enjoying himself the class still sing and dance and approve now watching them – John and PG do a turn and land up face to face – sound level of class drops as they move closer – class changes from sound to mime of kissing and sex and words of egging him on – John and PG find a very tender spot of communication (eyes, physical) which John cannot handle and pulls away to go back to his work – the class loudly mocks him and John walks back to the table to work. The class breaks up – chattering in groups – someone – P3 – approaches John kindly)

P3      Hintoni ngo ku, yeka lento watu bizi apo. (John just stares blankly at him) Ma siye mtyanam su yenza ndjalo. (calls to pupil P4 to help him) He! wena Steve, zwakala, thetha opa

P4      Wena John. O diragni ha. Pakama o danse le tsona

JM      (crossly) I dont understand Zulu man

P4      (laughing) Gasi si Zulu. Ke si Tswana.

(class all laugh)

P3      (gesticulates to pupil 1 – the earth lady – to come over and help)

P1      Yebo buti.

JM      Hey you Lady, I told you I do not understand Zulu

P1      Awuzwa ukuthi lomfana uthini. Uyazi yin? Lo mfana akafuni kulakla. (turns to class) Usisphuku phuku

| | |
|---|---|
| Class | (laughing) Usisphuku phuku (derides him – teases him – begin to crowd round his table jostling him – the forcible love girl tries to protect him -) |
| PG | Hey he is only trying to work – let him work |
| Class | Lets work him – we are going to sculpt him |

(they grab John and place him on the table – we hear shouts of no and be careful and then just Hey Hey from him and the singing and merry shouting from them – they start the Forcible Love song but no snake dancing only they carry the table (with John on it trying to keep his balance some way) they put the table down and John is there shielding himself with hands over his face – not looking – protecting -they all begin dancing – this time a sort of thumping war dance – a zulu war dance and chanting and one person gets onto to the table with John and begins sculpting him – his hands are left in the position of shielding, or made more emphatic to ward off the blows (opposite to the hands of the teachers 'sculpture' when the class began – there must be a recollection and poignancy here)

(Dancing of the full cast – but into a Zulu frenzy – this can include the entire cast – but not in Kuanyama dress) – It must end in a Rorke's Drift battle freeze and the Voice enters:

| | |
|---|---|
| Voice | That was the start. At Rorke's Drift, John was institutionalized for manic depression – a clinical name for madness. His big booming laugh and poet's personality could never cover the split in his mind that surfaced at Rorke's Drift.<br>He was found, running up a mountain, naked, screaming in Oshikwanyama. He could not relate you see – a Kuanyama amoungst Zulu's (the cast starts clicking their fingers and continues until the end of the scene) in an English (PG sings Forcible) province (the cast sings Love). |

(all we hear now is the clicking and Forcible Love song with the entire cast singing it not divided in male and female – the cast slowly exits)

| | |
|---|---|
| | A (slide of Lonely Man 1974 [Lev.69]) lonely man, happy in his art work. Lonelyness – look at this picture. The artist, happy, yet lonely. Happy to create and produce and lonely because he cannot join in the social fun around him. John recovered from this first bout of madness – carving cups and making tea trays for the nursing sisters at the Madedeni hospital – the Mental Hospital at Newcastle |

Finally, John returned to Odibo where he taught art. (slide of Our Schools 1980 [Lev.159]) our schools need art" (pause) and he worked on his craft.

Pause – blackout – sounds of work on stage – and a crash

# Scene Eight: The Ford 250

John rushes in screaming – running around the stage – then calls –

JM              Father – father (screams and shouts – rushes around) father – father (the father rushes in very worried – half dressed as if about to go to Church)

JM              something bad has happened

F               What is it John.

JM              Accident, accident (screams)

F               (very concerned) Are you all right. Is anyone hurt

JM              Yes – yes my car

F               Whom – where – I will get the doctor (turns to rush off)

JM              my ford – it is no good.

F               (turning back) John was anyone hurt

JM              Yes – the king – the kingpins of the car

F               (realising) John, I must go to church now – but tell me later

(JM sits down – thinks – takes linocut and begins working furiously on the Ford 250, 1973 [Lev.46] speaks the text of FORD 250 as he is working)

JM              John Muafangejo bouth a Ford 250 for R1000.00 on 12/2/73. It was a very good second hand car. This motor cas was Fetus Shanikos but he sold it to me on 17/2/73 – the car was soldered by Fetus worker at Oshakati garage on left hand kingpin caps. On 23/2/73 the Ford went through the border into Angola. This was caused by the soldered

29

King pin caps which again aplit and the wheel got off. My students, my driver and I nearly killed in this accident because Festus deceived me by selling me a car which is out order. I took the car back to him on 26/2/73 so that he can just bring my money back. It was my first car which I bought. Ford 250 custom

(as he is busy working we feel a presence overlooking him – can be a light shining down next to him – depends on the visualisation of the voice character)

Voice:  The text starts on the left hand side – why is he working on the right hand side, backwards. When you cut a graphic – a lithograph, an etching you have to engrave it backtofront, upside down, like mirror writing. This is because when you print it – it comes out reverse, the right becomes left and left becomes right, black becomes white and white becomes black. You can all try it at home tonight, take a potato, cut it in half, carve something on it, ink it up and print it on a paper, not the best silk table cloth mind you. Not yet. Anything perhaps newspaper, like John. Any if you are really daring use linoleum – -and take care with the writing. If you try and write as much as John did – your whole life's story (flash on slide of Zimbabwe House 1975 [Lev.107]) it is all in mirror writing (laughs) – hard hard hardwork,(pause) doing art. (exits at the same time as the father returns – again some recognition or force field of communication

F  (returning and seeing the work) Looks at work - (laughs – John laughs too) you lose your car John but look you get a Ford 250 Custom- that is that you must call it (they both laugh)

JM  (places lino in mirror gesture to that of his mother when she clasped him to her heart –  scene 2 – when they met) father (pause) father – I want to learn – I want to go to High places I want to go to University father – I want to learn I want to be educated to university – the University of cape (slight pause) cape town

F  But you have learnt John

JM  Noooo

30

| | |
|---|---|
| F | But you have John |
| JM | Noo (pleadingly) father |
| F | John you have what you have – do your art and you will learn and we all will learn |
| JM | Father they tell me that Cape Town University is good school – there is a good art school there – that is the best art school – I want to learn more power father – they will accept me for I want to learn Father (clasps the father) |
| F | (holding John 1/2 pleased; 1/2 exasperated) John I shall write to them and see if they will accept you |

## Scene Nine: University of Cape Town

(John remains nervously walking around about to be interviewed, the father exits as the first of the interviewers walks on shouting, Optional Slide: An Interview at Cape town University, 1971 [Lev.38]).

| | |
|---|---|
| Interv. | Next (the interviewers all file in – take their places – imaginary pens and papers, forms |
| Interv. | Are you John Muafangejo |
| J | Yes, yes |
| Interv. | I see from your application form that you would like to come and study here at the University – why have you chosen us and not another one |
| J | What you say |
| Interv. | (slowly) You have applied for this university - why |
| J | It is good to be learnt. I want to learn more so that I can teach. I want to learn. I am an artist of S.W. Africa. The Anglican artist who is very interesting in Art work for his life. I am always busy doing art in different things. I can say I like to study art more again until I get Diploma or Degree in Art (snort from interviewer) You have all many |

31

|  | pens – can I have one too (grabs a pen from an interviewer and looks at it) – it is good to make art eh. |
|---|---|
| Interv. | Where did you study for your profession as an artist. |
| J | I am yours faithfully artist |
| Interv. | If you are an artist why did you apply to this university (John does not reply) |
| Interv. | Do you think people in this institution will accept your work because you are a black artist |
| J | I dont know because I am not black art – I paint so I come here to learn |
| Interv. | why do you only use black paint |
| J | why - it is cheap. The colour is in the work not in the paint |
| Interv. | You were in Rorkes drift and you were also learning weaving and some painting. But you did not know the language so how did you communicate with the people there |
| J | I use my hands to do my work |
| Interv. | John why did they put you in the hospital |
| J | Really I dont know – I was only just feeling tired – ya it was just like a dream to me. |
| Interv. | (aggressively) Why were you in the mental hospital |
| J | I was mad |

(interviewers react nervously)

| Interv. | but you are not mad |
| J | I was never mad (slaps the interview table or some object) – even now I am not mad |
| Interv. | Do you think your people like your "art" |

| J | my past life – I dont think so – I dont know |
|---|---|
| Interv. | Do you have friends – a girlfriend |
| J | I am just busy with my work so I have no time |

(Interviewers are now restless and want to terminate the interview)
> so my whole interest is in my work and to teach. You see
> my point is – you will do that

(some of the interviewers begin to leave,)

> but ah there will be times

(the Interviewers gradually leave him – obviously going to give a no
recommendation, John is left speaking/crying out this speech)

> when you doing this for somebody and when you are doing
> this for yourself – you see actually maybe it can be your
> mother died actually and you want to tell somebody about
> it then you will draw a picture how you mother died and
> when you are doing this for yourself you just maybe draw a
> simple picture

(everyone has left by now)

> you understand what I am saying (turns to audience)
> I think it is like someone who sings a song just to write to
> us what I am feeling to express myself or to interpret my
> inner feelings (the which doctor enters and stalks John) to
> the people.

(Spot on voice or blackout)

(Meanwhile the rest of the cast take positions – in the centre is the bishop
who stands with his back to the audience – on the ground in front of him is
John on his back being held down by the whichdoctors assistant and the
whichdoctor whereever he finds himself will jump around the stage –
leapfrogging until he gets to John and his assistant when he throws the bones
and begins the next scene – the cast half Kuanyamas and 1/2 in priest cloth
(the straightjacket) intermingle with each other along either side of and the
John the priest, they form two lines interleading inwards where if the line
were extended would be to the bishop – they face alternatively to the front
and and away – they will each turn at the points when the bishop and the
whichdoctor swop around

See notes for diagram to this scene[2]

Voice      (rising voice to mirror ealier rising of voice)
The university of Cape Town said no. No! John's work was being exhibited all over the world but the University of Cape Town said No.
John's mother died. He wanted to return to his home across the border on the Angolan side of the Kuanyama tribe for his mother's funeral – the war and politics said no. As he wrote: The war stopped me to go to one I love The Bishops whom he also loved needed to return to the mission, but the government said no and expelled them out of the borders of the country.
John tried to continue his work at Odibo, but the army burnt down the houses and the printing press was ruined. So again no.
But John never accused – never identified a culprit for the source of his frustrations. When the mission house was bombed and razed to the ground, he cut the story into the linoleum saying the responsible party was "Mr No (pause)body". "Mr Nobody. Mr Nobody.
But, some-body arrested the artist, put him in chains – for all the no's in his life – yeses to him – were driving him once more into madness.

(Optional Slides Detail: No body 1975 [Lev.114]and Artist in chains 1975 [Lev.107])

## Scene Ten: The Which doctor

(The whichdoctors assistant holds john down who is struggling and thrashing about. The whichdoctor is crouching and moving about – jumping – a different type of thrashing about repeating all sorts of sounds including Kwata nawa – he pulls out the bag of bones and throws them – for the rest of the cast see above and glossary they remain immobile)

Whitchdoctor  Kwata nawa kadona kamge. Wakwamungo tawa tingeyioi
Adu, adu, adu, adu adu adu
Adu Adu Adu adu adu adu

---

[2]   The diagrammatic notes here were lost, orde Oxford 2014

(Much thrashing about and looking at the bones and Adu adu etc then he falls on his back almost parallel to John (who is on his back and the assistant holds down his hand (as she is holding down John's hand – a different type of they are holding hands – but the connection/joining must be clear

Assist          Onganga ofayiti kelela ota aiya paife.
                Ikulombweke kutya oto vele shike
                Ikulombweke kutya oto vele shike

Whichdoctor     (gets up from trance, the assistant gathers up the bones)
                You are mad – John Muafangejo (the assistant flees and as
                she leaves the bishop-back to audience – takes up a
                position – the scene that follows has the two switching
                round – they are two halves of John – and should revolve –
                at one point the couching whichdoctor stands and the
                priest slowly becomes 'smaller' and at one of these points
                when the priest is crouching the whichdoctor removes the
                cross and puts it in his bag of bones
Whichdoctor     – you are mad (whichdoctor and bishop switch around –
                bishop now faces the audience and John)

B               (chanting and in a singsong voice) Artist was arrested in 9th
                of August in 1975

W               Artist was tied arms and legs with chains by somebody

B               and sent me to Onekuaja

W               Kuanyama which doctor to give me some medicine for 7
                days

(the following words which are underlined are echoed by the cast as John gets
up and speaks)

JM              They were said that John was <u>sick</u> for <u>mad</u> but there were
                just <u>worried</u> me too much and I was <u>talking</u> too much
                mostly reading bible <u>singing</u> and praying because I was
                <u>lonelyness</u>

(this is repeared by all for a little while)

                they were talking lie to say I was mad man. I was worried.

(now running around the stage)

35

it gets awfully <u>lonely</u>,
lonely;
like screaming,
<u>screaming</u> lonely;
screaming down dream alley,
screaming <u>blues</u>, like none can hear;
but you hear clear and loud:
<u>echoing</u> loud;
like it's for you.
I talk to <u>myself</u> when I write,
shout, scream to myself;
then back to myself
<u>scream</u> and shout
<u>shouting</u> a prayer,
<u>screaming</u> noises,
knowing this way I tell
the world about what still lives;
even maybe
just to scream and shout.
of lonelyness

(collapses – all freeze)

(Optional Slide Detail I was lonelyness 1975 [Lev.107]

Voice:          John, unable to work in the war torn North,(Kuanyamas
                leave) came to Windhoek (Anglicans leave) and started
                work in the St George's Diocese. Happy productive years –
                free accommodation from the Diocese. Money from
                exhibitions, generous help from interested parties and
                other artists, international exposure eventually enabled
                John to buy a house in Katutura. With his new found fame,
                came the articles – Times, Advertiser, Republikein,
                Namibian, Observer, the German newspapers,
                international press and the interviews -
                But maybe (pause) maybe that is just what I saw, from
                my perspective (pause) from what I had read – maybe
                overall this fame was fame(pause) politics and
                circumstances (pause) and the art – the art was not seen –
                not appreciated if you like – besides there were now, there
                were now, new conflicts that this Windhoek dweller had to
                deal with –

(all exit and the sound of music is heard)

# Scene Eleven: Tuyeniko elonga

(Music is heard off stage – playing of the Kalimba which is carried by two people and one is playing it. Cast comes in swaying and working along the lines of digging/ grooving a linocut (ie enlarged/distorted movements of creating a linocut – again the women sing separately from the men and then all join in – the c=cast but not John)

C-F         Tuyeni ko

C-M         Tuyeni ko elonga

C-F         Tuyeni ko

C-M         Tuyeni ko elonga

C-F         Tuyeni ko

C-M         Tuyeni ko elonga

C-All       Tuyeni tuyeni tuyeni ko elonga (all are-on stage with John admiring them and looking at them as if they were pictures – at the one side is a table and chair – same spot as where it was during the Rorkes drift scene with the art teacher – the Kalimba is in the place where the whichdoctor/bishop were standing – as john goes to sit at the desk one of the cast breaks away and singing the words goes up to John – at his desk once finished their words they rejoin the line of the Kalimba by flowing into the swaying grooving movements – each cast member does this as they sing their number – all the time the Kalimba is playing softly)

C1          At first you need linoleum (holding in front - echoes of Ford 250 position)-not too small – he liked it large (places it against table)

JM          (not singing, plain speaking – picks up lino and places it on table) I am a Kuanyama of the Owambo people of Namibia.

C2          Now you have to do some work and its special work, cutting work (carries imaginary lino-cutter) and what you need is a lino-cutter (puts it on table)

| | |
|---|---|
| JM | The border between Angola and Namibia divides our tribe. |
| C3 | The thing you need is a tin of ink (carrying imaginary tin) – not any ink – only black ink – black ink (gives it to John) |
| JM | (opening imaginary tin) I looked after cattle, calves and goats between nine to thirteen. |
| C4 | To get the ink out of the pot you have to use a spatula (gives imaginary spatula) |
| JM | (digging out – echoes the movements of the group) First I was carving wooden cups and snakes when I was 24 years old. |
| C5 | Now at last the thing you need is a roller (rolling movements with imaginary roller) - a roller is what you need |
| JM | (taking roller and rolling) Then Minister Mallory saw my talent and I went from the small village in the North of South West Africa to the mission Art School at Rorkes Drift. |
| C6 | (holding up with two fingers imaginary paper) and now you need ah ah paper – to put over your board |
| JM | (placing paper on board and standing) I will be the first professional african artist in SWA |
| C7 | At last you need a spoon – not to deep and not to flat – just a spoon to rub it over with – oh just like you are doing it now (all humming as John rubs the 'spoon' over the 'paper' and 'linoblock') |
| JM | If gods Will (John lifts the paper and the entire cast do likewise with their imaginary papers) I am happy, enjoyable man in his art work daily. |

Kalimba music stops.

| | |
|---|---|
| C7 | (who has remained at the table) Hope (pointing to John) and Optimism (pointing to the cast) |
| All | (except John and C7) in spite of present difficulties |

(Optional Slide: Hope and Optimism 1984 [Lev.209])

JM                There are just two great human needs, light on the mystery of life and life for the mastery of life. I am with god (picks up imaginary completed work and places it above the Kalimba instrument as if hanging it there – the scene now dissolves into the exhibition scene – it is important that the movements and attitudes of the cast change from the melody of dance and creativeness to that of the business of an exhibition)

## Scene Twelve: The Exhibition Scene

(cast now become viewers and an exhibition – referred to as 'V' viewers)

VI                Mmmmmm – its beautiful

V2                Yes is it not – wow it is quite beautiful

V3                Darling what is his name

V4                er, ah (takes out imaginary magnifying glass and looks at bottom right hand corner) John Mufangi-jo (cast begins a high pitched version of Tuyeni ko elonga – as they dress themselves in fine garments to show off for the exhibition opening – when all have dressed themselves accordingly the opening begins – John is standing to the side of the opening speaker V4)

V4                (moves to the front and taps imaginary microphone a few times) Testing, testing, please One two three, een, twee, drie, eins – no good – this thing is not working – (turns) well since we have a failure here I hope you can all hear me speaking without a microphone. Tonight is a very special night – I would like to welcome you all to the opening of this exhibition of pictures by the very talented (forgets name) er ah (calls John over who whispers in his ear)John Muafangejo (John beams - nothing malicious or upset from John at all in this scene - takes it all in his happy and humble stride) who is here with us tonight (short, polite and discrete applause from the viewers) and without further ado I'd like to ask our special guest speaker Mr

|     |                                                                                                        |
|-----|--------------------------------------------------------------------------------------------------------|
|     | Christopher Till to open this exhibition (a viewer comes forward)                                       |
| VI  | Thankyou - ladies and gentlemen this exhibition here stands today as an autobiography of a perceptive and visionary artists. Mr John Muafangejo |
| V4  | (inter-rupts) second speaker (VI remains front of stage and chatters away gesticulating - the intention being that after all the speakers have opened there is a tower of bable type noise of voices) |
| V2  | (comes to front) There is not much I can add to what has already been said about John Muafangejo and his work |
| V4  | (inter-rupts) Third speaker (as with second speaker)                                                   |
| V3  | John's art is in every way unique in Namibia - most artists illustrate in the main                     |
| V4  | (inter-rupts) fourth speaker (as with second/third speaker)                                            |
| V5  | Muafangejo's work reminds me in this respect of David Hockney - it is also                             |
| V4  | (inter-rupts) fifth speaker (as with second/third/fourth speaker)                                      |
| V6  | John Muafangejo is clearly a man divided - something which enriches his work rather than (by this stage the bable of voices is high) |
| V4  | (interrupts all - they stop and move back to their positions) So ladies and gentlemen I'd like to ask you all to come and sign our guestbook (the following visitors all sign the imaginary guestbook) |
| V1  | Pity there were not more postcards                                                                     |
| V2  | The black and white is too harsh for Sunday morning without breakfast                                  |
| V3  | I cry and pray for South Africa                                                                         |
| V5  | Left wing rubbish                                                                                       |

| V6 | Did he really do it with his toes |
|---|---|

V6        Did he really do it with his toes

V7        true what they say, simple is best

V8        is it love that brings us hope

V9        Enda naua John, Kalemga kale pamne naye

V10       it is work to inspire truth of feeling from artists instead of our usual technical dryness to achieve the balance is what we see here

V11       they cant segregate the black and white in their cuttings

V12       Like a black miro, simple canoletto but Klee shape, Piccasso syntax, child and form, understand Renoir heaven

V4       And so John - if I may call you so - we'd like to make you feel at home so we are going to sing you a song from your country (JM beams)

(All cast begin coughing in a theatrical way and clearing their throughts and begin to sing Tuyeni ko elonga completely out of key)

V-all     Tuyeni ko, tuyeni ko tuyeni ko elonga

V1 (detaching himself from the group approaches V4 - staggering a bit and slightly drunk - staggers around a bit and V4 is respectful as this is a potential client this section is all in mime – V1 hauls out a cheque book looks at 'picture' hanging above the Kalimba and begins to write out cheque - when the cheque is completed he staggers across - is about to give it to John - stops and gives it to the gallery owner and then walks over to the 'picture'. in the meantime the gallery owner tears a bit of the cheque and hands it to John at which point V1 lifts the 'picture' off [H1]the wall – smiles contentedly and begins walking off stage singing just Tukeni ko elonga whereupon the entire viewers pair up and dissapear singing tuyeni ko elonga leaving John, the Kalimba (and the two people holding it) on stage – John smiles and leaves and as he leaves the gallery owner re-enters and goes to the Kalimba at the position where the player of it was – looks at it and the two people holding it and has something in mind – then clicks his/her fingers and the Kalimba player comes on very excited as he/she thinks that he/she is going to be asked to play.

The gallery owner indicates that he/she must replace one of the people carry it – this he/she does not seem to understand until one of the carriers says:

Carrier I            Tambula Man. Oshiri oshiri
                     Ame ondaloloka payife oh
                     (Player as he/she takes over and carrier one is stalking off)
                     Haîxa ta ka hâ sasa ta kâ tani hâ o[3]
                     (The gallery owner now gets them to lower the Kalimba
                     and then stands on it indicating for them to carry him/her
                     off stage – as they are moving)

Carrier 2:           linima eyi yomapunua eyadi otee,
                     Oyi hole ashike omafano you yikatulike komakuma.
                     Iinima eyi oilai eyi

then the gallery owner begins to sing Tukeni ko elonga and as they move off stage we hear the singing descend and a loud crash as if the gallery owner has fallen)

Blackout and then John appears as if part of the audience – playing a part – there must be a change in tempo here to allow for the interview scene – tempo to imply a looking on into the stage which Jm and pressman no longer occupy – an imaginary screen can be put into place between them and the stage.

## Scene Thirteen: Pressman and John

P                    (arrives with briefcase and camera looking at watch – calls
                     out) Hullo John

JM                   Hullo

P                    (greets John, laughs, shakes hands – places briefcase down
                     – they both sit down – begins fiddling around with items)
                     How are you keeping

J                    Not so bad not so good

P                    And how is your work going
J                    I try to survive anyhow – I need materials

---

[3]        Nama

| | |
|---|---|
| P | materials – money |
| J | paper, ink, linocut, pens |
| P | You are doing a lot of work now |
| J | Yes |
| P | Do you mind if we make a taperecording - thats fine with you |
| J | No – I have no problem |
| P | ja (takes out taperecorder which John examines) |
| J | taperecording (laughs) no problem |
| P | and to take some photos |
| J | Photos (laughs) ah OK ah its a nice tape-recorder this – can you give ah me this one |
| - | -can I have it eh |
| P | (laughs – both laugh) it was a present – it was a present to me ah I cant give you a..present – |
| J | Oh you are a lucky guy – (laughs) hey if I would be me hey |
| P | laughs – |
| J | give it to me |
| P | laughs |
| J | straight |

P and J laughs

| | |
|---|---|
| P | laughing – it was a present – I cannot give a present away (flashes his camera on John – blackout except on Pressman who reminisces) |
| P | John's hands movements, he had very very incredable long |

fingers – (gets up moves – eventually to circle John) longer
fingers than than anyone of us here – very long fingers –
longer than mine – longer than yours (points to audience)
– typical sort of artists fingers – and he used it like ah – I
think it is a cliche but ah – broken wing of a bird – his
movements – it was very very expressive – but like his wrist
was almost broken – like this – he had this fluttering
movements – that that (flashlight on John)
(moves)
The last time that I saw John I went away and I thought we
had a bond – there was a bond – but then I went away
and I read up about the Owambo people and traditions
and history of the border and stuff like that and I
developed another picture of him in my head so when I
went to interview him again I was expecting him to do
these things that I have read – thats why I asked him
specific things – also I wanted him to fit into this mould
that I had created as a result of all my readings and
research – I wanted to push him push him to push him
because I found out about his madness his spells of
madness I wanted to push him I wanted to know what
madness was this – at that stage also I read an article about
Van Gogh and Van Gogh the latest classification was that
he had some some illness that forced him to produce a
picture and I knew that Muafangejo used to work –
sometimes used to work with a frenzy of productivity – so
so so I thought there was some link but I dont think it was
exactly like that it was
(flashligh)

P

As I knew John – there was a most important thing that I
can remember it was that and I wanted and I wanted and I
felt something of the man – here was a man – -a wounded
man – a troubled man and he was also a very sensitive man
although he had his contradictions and he spoke with a
booming voice and at times he could be very abrupt – he
was not – he was not insensitive – he could pick up the
smallest detail
(flashlight)

P

His religion, his religion me myself being a religious or
trying to be very religious – he was very religious and in
the terms it felt like he was backsliding, he was backsliding
– to me – During our talk a very outspoken man barged in.
He was a big talking activist – Swapo, Dapof Namduf or

44

whatever – the typical racist paratrooper. He kept
undermining our discussion machine-gunning the flow of
our conversation with a little arsenal or irrelevant political
unjustices. We were talking art and he could not
understand this. For him, art was only a propoganda tool.
In this lies the tragedy of Muafangejo. He felt and heeded
the spiritual call of beauty but he was wounded by the
spear of his times, ah yes it was you are the brother of the
revolution – that was the word that he used
(flashlight to audience – lights on again) and interviews

P        You have not got the mark

J        Mark

P        The ritual mark – on your face

J        Ah No

P        Why not

J        I'm Kuanyama, the Kuanyama's people are no marks

P        No mark

J        No, no (begins to get up and leave)

P        Where are you going ?

J        (Exits) Eh ?

P        Where are you going ?

J        (off stage) Eh, eh – I'll come back

P        Getting too personal?

J        (offstage) Personal

P        But I must know, I think it's necessary for me to
understand your art

J        (offstage) My art ?

P        And what do you say with your work?

| | |
|---|---|
| JV | (offstage) I'm, I'm preaching, (returns to the desk) I'm passing – a – message to the owner of that picture, to whom we going to sell it to, to buy it, that is a message in it (pause – laughs) |
| P | OK, tell me, how do you make – how do you make a linocut? |
| J | First of all I sketch it. |
| P | You think about it? |
| J | Ja, I think it and when I think about it and I sketch it, from sketches, straight to the lino (laughs). Ja, first of all, I must think the – the – the, the previous caller for the picture, like here,(pause laughs) |
| P | OK, so, so you get the idea |
| J | Yes |
| P | What gives you the idea? |
| J | It's natural – natural idea. |
| P | But, but what gives you the idea. Do you go to nature and you see the birds and then you think, or you see a man doing something. |
| J | Aa-ha |
| P | Someone is talking and then you think ah – this – or |
| J | Sometimes, I'm naturally self copying – just I use mostly – ah – imagination. Ja. When I see you like that -and I want to draw you, I will add the more – things – to make it more story, power story. |
| P | Ja (laughs) |
| J | Ja (laughs) |
| P | Ja (laughs) |

46

| | |
|---|---|
| J | Ja (laughs)<br>(pause) |
| P | Who do you like, who do you like as artists, the work that you think is good. |
| J | Ah, all art really is good, but you must make something which everybody can show it – what's taking place. Rather than to make your own, if your own art, if you are not a teaching art, you can do something and then nobody knows.<br>(pause) |
| P | who do you like? |
| J | I like anybody. |
| P | You like anybody? |
| J | Yes, because it's still art. They're saying something, you see. Only the mind is a teaching line, because you can see it – what's going on – and then the children can see it and follow it. (gets up and leaves at opposite end to the one he exited from in the beginning) |
| P | Where are you going, (gets up and follows) I forgot to ask you about your art. |
| J | Yes |
| P | How do you get the drawing onto the lino? |
| J | I am sorry |
| P | How do you get the drawing onto the lino? |
| J | What you say |
| P | How do you get the drawing onto the lino? |
| J | Ahmm-looking (exits). |
| P | (questioningly) looking (and exits following after John)<br>John wait |

(Pressman exits following in confusion, having left his tape-recorder and camera on the interview table)

## Scene Fourteen: ible and able

(two stage hands enter – placing furniture around – this can also be played in the audience eg putting up poster on wall and using imaginary cameras and recorders)

| | |
|---|---|
| R | Forcable |
| L | Forcible Love |
| R | I'm not quite sure what it means |
| L | Forcible Love – what does forcible love mean |
| R | yes I dont understand |
| L | forcible love. |
| R | love (pause) that can be forced |
| L | well yes I suppose in that sense (R picks up the microphone and thrusts into L's face, who reacts) – yes love that can be forced – a love that has its own force – it is a forcible love – a love that cannot |
| R | you mean forceful |
| L | no forcible not forceful |
| R | ible or able |
| L | ible – well to me it means a love that cannot be altered – love cannot be – cannot be – cannot be – an unstopable love |
| R | you mean irrisistable love |
| L | no becuase that means – that has different connotations – forcible love means love that is forcible love |
| R | you dont mean love that can be forced |

| | |
|---|---|
| L | no – just the opposite (grabs tape-recorder and begins to exit, with it) |
| R | force – a force that can squeeze water out of a sponge |
| L | (turning) just the opposite (exits – same side as when in interview John first exited) |
| R | so it cant be forced |
| L | (offstage) away from its love – |
| R | (fingering camera, picks it up – focuses on where John was sitting during the Interview) maybe this is a colloquial use of the term force |
| L | (offstage, but enters on the word love) forcible love (R takes photo with flashlight) no |
| R | (amused, tries to continue taking photos with flashlight) use it in some sentence – use it in some other context than love |
| L | I dont think there is such a word as forcible love anyway |
| R | so its a neologism – I see |
| L | you just made that word up – its a created word - all truth is – |
| R | (puts down camera) no one is going to know what it means |
| L | until the play explains it to them – |
| R | oh yes but until then |
| L | they can use their imagination |
| R | oh imagination – but if I use my imagination with that sort of thing – then I think about (laughs) then all that appears to me is that of the speech (pause) the quality of mercy is not forced (pause) Portia's speech – without the use of force – not forcable – able I think – able I think |

| | |
|---|---|
| L | well its the connotation of both (they now move to spot where originally 12 year old Ndevesia first met his mother in Namibia, after she had converted and continue talking) – in other words fossible love – the love of an artist – you either have it in you or you dont have it in you |
| R | what – in an artist for his art |
| L | (pause – gently) no well art itself – you are either capable of doing it or not – you cant force it – you cant force someone to become an artist – you also cant force a true artist not to be one – the art is forcible if you are an artist it is a forcible love – that will override like all things – it will override any hardships |
| R | you mean an overpowering love |
| L | No – what it is to be an artist – that is fossible love ya – maybe the hardships today are more psychological, love, guilt, reparation, friendships, maybe the fossible of the artist can only be a fossible love – if its a forceable ambition then its not an artist. But it being a fossible love that is difficult – because you find it difficult to say no to people because of the quality of love if you will |
| R | so forcible is used in a very ambiguious sense of the word meaning different things in different context |
| L/R | ya/well/no/fine |
| L/R//L-R | duality, multilayered |
| R | you need a play to explain what you mean – full of the meaning that one pours into it-onto it – into it (exits) L (gesticulates and exits) |

## Scene Fifteen: Mama Afrika

(Image must contain a number of friezes from his work – must have the representation of Mother and Child (Mother and child (either or all three of the Mother and Child works ie [Lev.29], [Lev.134] or [Lev.196] –using Ndevasia Muafangejo – woman with hand over stomach and protecting the child. There is also the mielie-stamper and most of the items used as props – General hive of activity three (or more) men sitting on a stool – they appear to be working with their hands and signing. John is working

at his desk – he does not sing – which is now centre
stage that is where the whichdoctor and bishop stood.
Scene opens with no visuals but the singing of

| | |
|---|---|
| Female | Mama Afrika. |
| Male | Mama Afrika. |
| All | Mama Afrika. Mama Afrika. Shilongo shamanguluka |
| All | Mama Afrika. Mama Afrika. Mama Afrika. Mama Afrika. Shilongo shamanguluka |
| All | (higher note) Mama Afrika. Mama Afrika. Mama Afrika. Mama Afrika. Shilongo shamanguluka |
| All | Mama Afrika. Mama Afrika. Mama Afrika. Mama Afrika. Shilongo shamanguluka |
| JM | (coughs – singing quietens down) – (coughs again and stops working), coughs once more and staggers to his feet – hand still on table of linocut – the singing stops). JM stands upright – humming tune of a passing on hymn begins – John staggers towards the audience and the exhibition of his work – some members of the cast mime the passing on – at least one gathering and one showing the symbolic way onwards of the soul to the other countries – John staggers past them – as he staggers past them a number of the cast steal some of the items and carry them offstage – the following must be stolen<br>– someone takes off framed picture from the wall and carries it off<br>– someone goes to his desk and rolls up a picture and carries it off<br>– someone carries off the drums -someone carries off the mileier stamper<br>all this the 12 year old Ndvesia watches – first Johns departure then the stealing – all watched with his eyes – not moving his head.<br>all walk back on as if nothing has happened. One of them approaches the table and cannot resist putting a small item in his pocket |
| Voice: | If he is talking of lonelyness (pause) was it because he did not have someone to show his pictures to or (pause) was he |

51

doing these pictures because he did not have anyone to talk
to – he was lonely – (pause) perhaps his only friends were
the pictures – (pause) so he did the pictures for(ce)(pause)
The cast break out into the Mama Afrika song – L/R enter
from opposite sides – meet in the middle – where the
original border line was drawn – bow – straighten and
bump into each other and cross over so L takes his place
on Right and R his on left – all move forward to take bow.

Fin

(curtain calls – if there are sufficient then the following can happen after the
first call – to mirror someone asleep in the audience – one of the cast remains
asleep on stage – another goes up to him and wakes him up calling –

Dancer          Penduka Mukwetu nvakofa asheke oshima shihole eemhofi
                eshi

Then bows – Mama Afrika, Zulu dance reprieves etc.

# Appendix 1: Glossary, Translations and Notes

**Names:**

| | |
|---|---|
| Ndevasia | You are nominated |
| Tate | Father |
| Tukondjeni | lets struggle |
| Mwalengokanja | likes talking |
| Emanguluko | freedom |
| Hafeni | Peace |
| Kushiva | to invite |
| Okushiva omunie | to invite someone |
| Tuyeni ko Elonga | Lets go to work |

**Musical instruments**

| | |
|---|---|
| Okambulumbubwa | musical bow instrument of the Kuanyamas |
| Kalimba or sanza Zylophone | type instrument made of nails and planks |

## Scene One: Bowman

Omwiya wange wa Nangolo wahola Ngishi-nande wemuhola nokumu laya. Shimbwidanga ya Ndamona ya Namutenya novana ya Nghishekwa na Malondo la Matondo lambadangela ohatunhu kaNgule na Taitama lohumshito lohDndonga GaMatope. Ndjaba mutwe ya Nangolo yoo Shingwadja shikwiyu ya Mwahafa Hamunime, Okaima kada-lwa ohapofi kadalwa phapamhadali okatwika mesho namwengu kamena tete eumbinga omatwi inaa mbaduka

[My belt of Nangolo, who fell in love with Nghitundande, fell in love with her and crazily coveted her. shimbwidanga of Ndamona [I have seen] of Namutenya [day time] and her children of Nghishekwa [I will never be chaste] of Malondo who loitered near the ant-hill of Nghule and Taiama, the easterner of Ondonga [a village] of Matope. The head-of-elephant of Nngolo of Shingwadja – Shikwiya of Mwahafa [happy nation]. Hamunime [a lion], the little poor born-blind, the poor born scavenger, a blind-wild-spirit who got bear horn first, while the ears are still only buds.]

### Words which are used as nouns

| | |
|---|---|
| Omwiya | belt |
| Ndamona | I've seen |
| Namutenya | day time |
| Ndhishwhwa | I will nevever be chaste |
| Ondonga | a village |
| Mwahafa | happy nation |

Hamunmise                    a lion

## Scene Two: Efundula Ceremony
It is the intention of this scene to evoke something that is cultural and central
to the 'lost/past' origins of the artist thus the scene selected in the Namibian
context (as will be explained below) is the Efundula ceremony, it may be that
such a ceremony would be impossible to perform with actors who are not
Kuanyamas (I think not – as it will be an exercise in research and training
perhaps not unlike a Namibian actor's efforts in learning and performing
Shakespeare – whom I love) and if so it is within the scope of intention of the
playright to allow this scene to be altered entirely in form (not conceptual
content) to fit in with the traditional culture of another venue – eg if
performed in Barceleno perhaps there is a ritual ceremony of the Basques that
would be appropriate.

There is very little still written on the Kuanyama tribe and former Kuanyama
kingdom. The major material appears to me to be the following:

1. *The Native Tribes Of SWA,*-H.P. Smit, Cape Times, Cape Town, 1928

2. *In Feudal Africa,* Edwin M.Loeb, Mouton and Co, Indiana University
Research Centre in Anthropology, Folklore and linguisitics, 1962
- an excellent book

3. *The Ethnography of South Western Angola,* Carlos Estermann, Ed. Gordon
D Gibson, Africana Publishing Company, London, 1976

4. *Hair-styles and Head-dresses and ornaments in SWA/Namibia and Southern
Angola,* A Scherz, I.R. Scherz, G. Taapopi, A Otto, Gamsberg Publishers,
Windhoek, 1981 -an excellent book

5. *The Kuanyama of South West Africa,* J.P. Bruwer, M.A. Dissertation, no
further information at present.

6. Various journals, for examples
i) Efundula; The Initiation ceremony of the Kuanyama tribe', Walter Louw,
SWA Annual, SWA Publications, Windhoek, pp.124-27
ii) 'Can the living in Angola explain the past in Rhodesia', C.E. Fuller,
African Studies, Witwatersrand University, Johannesburg, Vol 11, 1952,
pp.182-89
The Efundula ceremony is chosen, not only as it fits in with a theme
examined, the culture 'clash' and that its composition lends itself to dramatic
interpretation but also that there is a strong link to another theme
detah/life/reborn and in Kuanyama culture there is a death and burial linkage

54

to the Efundula ceremony. Loeb (In Feudal Africa, Op. cit. p. 243-244)
writes:
'Upon the Efandula ceremony more than upon anything else in Kuanyama
culture tribal life depends' and the '...efundula was a chief cause of strife
between the native Christians and the pagans....the missionaries will not
allow the Christian natives even to witness it.'


**Scene seven: Forcible Love**

Pupil 1          Sa-ukebona buti. Kunjani
                 Hullo brother. How are you.
                 Uphumaphi wena. Mina ngiphuma kwa Zulu (or Durban).

                 Where do you come from. I'm from Durban.
                 Woza siye e Patini.
                 Lets go to the party

JM               I dont understand Zulu. Leave me. I'm busy working

Pupil 1          Uyazi yini.

                 Forcible Love.

Pupil 3          Hintoni ngo ku, yeka lento watu bizi apo. Ma siye
                 mtyanam su yenza ndjalo. (calls pupil 4 to help him) He!
                 wena Steve, zwakala, thetha opa

                 Whats wrong now, leave the work and lets go my friend.
                 Dont be like that. Hey! You Steve, come here and talk
                 here.

Pupil 4          Wena John. O diragni ha. Pakama o danse le tsona

                 You John. What are you doing. Stand up and dance with
                 us.

                 (laughing) Gasi si Zulu. Ke si Tswana.

                 (laughing) It is not Zulu. It is Tswana

Pupil 1.         Yebo buti.

                 Hey brother

Pupil 1    Awuzwa ukethi lomfana uthini. Uyazi yin? Lo nifana
           akafuni kulakla. Usisphuku phuku

           Dont you hear what this guy says. Do you know what?
           This guy dont want to listen. You fool.

## Scene ten: The Which doctor

Whitchdoctor    Kwata nawa kadona kamge. Wakwamungo tawa tingeyioi
                Adu, adu, adu, adu adu adu

                Hold him tight my girl. What is that the spirits saying. Adu
                Adu Adu adu adu adu

The Girl    Onganga otayiti kelela ota aiya paife.
            The which doctor says wait. He will come now
            Ikulombweke kutya oto vele shike
            He is coming to tell you what you sickness is
            Ikulomfoweke kutya oto vele shike
            He is coming to tell you what you sickness is

## Scene twelve: Exhibition

V9    Tuyeni ko elonga
      lets go to work

      enda naua John, Kalemga kala pamne naye
      safe journey John, god be with you /Goodbye John god be
      with you.

Usher I    Tambula Man. Oshiri oshiri
           Hold (get) it Man. For sure for sure
           Ame ondaloloka payife
           oh I'm now damn tired

Usher 2    Haîxa ta ka hâ sasa tâ ka tani hâ o[4].
           I would have been angry if I was supposed to carry you

Usher 3:    (takes over from usher 2)
            Iinima eyi yomapunua eyadi otee,
            These fucking boors – stomachs full of tea

---

[4]    Nama

Oyi hole ashike omafano you yikatulike komakuma.
They admire pictures to be hung on the wall
linima eyi oilai eyi
they are numbskull

## Scene fifteen: Mama Afrika[5]
Mama Afrika. Mama Afrika. Mama Afrika.
Shilongo shamanguluka
Mother Afrika. Mother Africa Mother Africa
Our country. It is free

## Curtain call
Kuanyama (Sleeping)
Kuanyama Penduka Mukwetu nvakofa asheke oshima shihole eemhofi eshi
Get up my friend. you you nonsense you like sleeping

## Notes
The author is grateful to the following authors, translators and publishers for
permission to include the poems etc in this play:

Requiem by Verdi; *The Paradox* by Francesca Pereira; Lonely by Bloke
Modisane, Pedro Vorster for the extracts from the unpublished interview
between himself and John Muafangejo.

The author acknowledges the assistance and help in the workshoping process
of the NTN, the actors and all staff of the MTN and of the director Terence
Zeeman. Without their assistance this version would not have been possible.
It must also be stated that in the workshopping process the technical
assistance and advice of persons like Mark Behrens (lighting) and Rita Louise
Hofmeyr, Mark Behrens and Terence Zeeman (sound) and Katja Homchen
and the cast as a whole (research and costumes were all indispensable. To all
these persons many thanks.

First performance of Forcible Love (NTN version) was held on 21 March
1991 at the National Theatre of Namibia with the following cast:

Producer: NTN.
Director: Terence Zeeman
Artistic Director: Orde Levinson

---

5  Note declensions. Emanguluko. means freedom, shi = our; sha = it is; manguluka = it is
  liberted, it is already free

Cast in alphabetical order:

| NTN Company | Dancers |
|---|---|
| Allen Ambor | Sain Amukaku |
| Naomi Beukes | Gissela Antonius |
| Patrick Blaauw | Victoria Benjamin |
| Daphne de Klerk | Monica David |
| Marfha Hashikutuva | Lidia Frans |
| Nonnan lob | Titos Jonas |
| Simon Kapenda | Fetus Nelumbu |
| Benito Maniarengane | Josephine Nghhangaabo |
| Danny Matroos | Emille Nghidinbwa |
| David Ndjavera | Libgrtlna Nghkevaly |
| Lucky Pieters Moses Paulus | |
| Banana Shekupe | Lazarus Shalukeni |
| Pedro Yorster | Simon Simon |
| Patricia Viisani | Lonia Shimmwandi |
| Mees Xteen | |

Special thanks to the John Muafangejo Foundation for permission to use items in copyright, the slides of the work of John Muafangejo,, and text from his writings.

**Poems used in Forcible Love (NTN version)**

1.

> The cross, the icon
> The disciples fought
> They are still fighting
> The whiteman claims
> His god supreme
> And blackman muses

White god, in reason can I hope for grace bestowed,
The disciples fought. They are still fighting, maybe
Somewhere in white clouds, somewhere in blackest
Abyss, the white god and the black god dumb,

> Look silently on
> The disciples fought
> They all of them join
> Battle, fierce raging,
> Each god is mighty.

They must be. It must be. The world is constant in its chaos.
The world is crumbling and all gods are silent. Evil begets
Good begets evil. Watching. Wenching Eves, empty headed apes

58

Demanding, exacting. Their folly drowning in spirits flowing.

> And the Infant, crying
> For the dried-up stream
> The lapped-up stream
> Caked stream of life
> Is milked in a manger
> Sawdust and straw.
> Cool breeze fleeting
> Past suspense, hope,
> And prophecy. Empty.

The age old tree without, magnificent, proudly stands
Its yellowing leaves waft to and fro against the deep
Blue sky. The mind persists in calmness, and frenzy
Beats a wild resounding drum within the tortured heart.

> Learn patience
> O frenzied drumbeat
> Be still and rein
> Thyself. Advent of
> Destiny. Wildly yours.
> Then canst thou beat
> Wild wild refrain
> And drum and dance
> For joy. Or rend
> Dumb heavens with
> Thy woes. The age
> Old tree, the cheery
> Room, the bright blue
> Sky above. The drum
> Still blind, beats on.

The fevered drum still blind beats wildly fiercely on.
No crumbs fall from the orgies of the rich. Eves and apes
With licentious smell trampling the earth.
Under their feet the bones of infants. Disciples still
Fighting. Each god is mighty. The world is crumbling. And gods are silent.

THE PARADOX by Francesca Yetunde Pereira.

2.

> it gets awfully lonely,
> lonely;
> like screaming,

screaming lonely;
screaming down dream alley,
screaming blues, like none can hear,
but you hear clear and loud:
echoing loud;
like it's for you.
I talk to myself when I write,
shout, scream to myself;
then back to myself
scream and shout
shouting a prayer,
screaming noises,
knowing this way I tell
the world about what still lives;
even maybe
just to scream and shout.
is it I lack the musicians contact
direct?
the smell of human bodies;
or, is it true, the writer
creates
(except the trinity with God,
the machine and He)
incestuous silhouettes
to each other scream and shout,
to me shout and scream
pray and mate;
inbred deformities of loneliness?

Lonely by Bloke Modisane

**Slides Used:**
1.      L – Kuanyama Wedding [Lev.34]
        R – Old Fashion [Lev.204]
2       L – Kuanyama wedding [Lev.41]
3       L – She is divorcing her husband [Lev.161]
        L – They are longing each other [Lev.179]
4.      L – Bishop [Lev.28]
        R – Confirmation [Lev.162]
        L – The baptised of Christ [Lev.9]
        R – Confirmation [Lev.162]
5       L – Unity is strengeth [Lev.260]
6.      R – Love is approaching [Lev.66]
        L – Lonely Man – man of man [Lev.69]
        L – Our schools need art [Lev.159]

7.      L – Ford 250 [Lev.46]
        R – Zimbambwe House [Lev.107]
8.      L – Whichdoctor [Lev.142]
        R – Self [Lev.8]
9.      R – Hope and Optimism [Lev.209]
10      L – Kudu Friends [Lev.138]

# Appendix 2: Publicity/Other Material Relevant to the First Performance

## THE NAMIBIAN – FAX 33980

It took a Norwegian Journalist by the name of Inge Trondsen, who was on a months visit to Namibia to study Amateur Theatre and culture here to open my eyes (and many others) and smell the roses. I have been in the Country for the last ten years and have never bothered about finding out about other cultures, much to my shame. You see, most of us ex-South Africans (and Namibians) are using up too much time dwelling on our own private bitterness to take the time of day and find out about other cultures.

Well! The play "Forcible Love", a musical drama, based on the life of the Namibian Artist John Muafangejo was a "forcible" introduction into one of such cultures. For the hour and a half that the play was on, I was living and experiencing a bit of the artist's happiness, pain and suffering. A bit of love and bonding. I had this desire to get on stage and join in with the dancing, to protect the child, and then the man, to clap my hands with happiness and then weep with sadness and loneliness.

Where were we? So powerful was the play! I do sincerely hope that representatives of the Ministry of Education, Culture and Sport were there to see it. This play should be funded by Government and be allowed to tour. Not only in Namibia but outside of its borders, so that others can also experience and get a glimpse of Namibian culture. Maybe the cast could put on a private show for our President Dr Sam Nujoma and some of the Diplomatic Corps.

My heartfelt thanks to the Cast? Director, Script writer and all those that helped to make it happen.

cc = The Director, T Zeeman
Script Writer, O Levinson

How be Ordephus in the underworld, tickling the vocals chords of the cardboard cast and making the quick to spit tongues in the seats, sarcastic paper scripters sing and rhymn In praise of your omnipotent dialogue and inventive scenarios ? I hope this is the case, Paul. GOOD LUCK, look forward to seeing it on vid.

# HARD WORK TO BE AN
# ARTIST ᓍᓍᓍ! 17-03-91

The Artists N.T.N

　　　　　Its been a please and
honour to allow ~~you~~ me work hand
in hand with you Although it may seem
to you that I was Just like a passenger
in a bus ~~full~~ of drivers or mechanics.
Never the less I've learnt and gained
alot of things I didnt Know ~~Before~~
and Indeed all this was through your
Cooperation Lives and I hope it will still live
in you through you lovely Good Director
Terence. I would say Ive proved hime the
best in and Out. having seen the produc
-n you working on and then if I turn to
the Director I hope you would allow and
help me praise him to say he very good
For many books in theatre say Africa
theatre is one of the most difficult to
direct especially for foreigners but in
his cas he has enought time to trouble
himself to teach us and promote our own
Culture through that which I would say
its really rearly done by other White
Directors.

　　　　　In the other hand Mr. T.
Leeman sees no Colour be ~~you~~ white
~~Black~~ white gray if youre and this
is what makes him a great director Simply
because he has Qualities of being a ~~is~~ Leader
and not a Boss I hope most of you
Know the differences between a Boss and

A Leader. For a boss will always want the following—

- A Boss will Command
- A Boss will Consider himself first
- A Boss wants to be ~~feared~~ etc.

But A Leader will:

- Show by example
- Consider others or his people first
- Will always want to be Close to his ~~people~~ everytime when neccessary, etc.

For above ~~-facts~~ of being a leader I ~~woda~~ ~~Say~~ I Envy Terence ~~and~~ his good Leadership ~~that~~ Unites us together.

Coming to Descipline I would Say descipline has no end but depending ~~of what~~ on the particular organisation and Society so in this ~~respect~~ I'm proud to write you that I've never Seen and never experienced a big Club with great respect like that I mean what makes up the Club ~~ase~~ people and ~~you~~ being the ~~people~~ I would say keep on with that respect. Theatre is something really good and with a clean future and through it we shall no our Identity and for Sure no Artist in theatre will give up his Identity and Culture

THEATRE FOR CUTURAL AND NATIONAL IDENTITY. So through that play you Can See what respect Terence has for Other Cultures, lets thank him please. Well I'm writing this not to praise

12

③ him but to make it clear to some of us who are still doubting of him.

Now I thank you once more for the Welcome and Hospitality presented to me I really enjoyed the last part of my Stay because of you So in this respect I would Say God be with you and Continue with all the best for the Sky is the Limit.

Many, many, many regards to a actors and all members of N.T.N staff So Iah Guide Iah bless. Loving you always.

~~Sitmbeko~~

Terence. S. MUYUNDA

you Can Contact me through the ~~following~~ Address bellow

THE DIRECTOR,
KAOMA ARTS THEATRE,
P.O. Box 940112,
KAOMA. (West field)
ZAMBIA.

Sorry for all the bad things I've done to the Club and if any it was all by not knowing my apology extends to all Individuals of N.T.N. for those who Intead to visit me you are welcome and Can Inform me a month or two months in advance. Chao

Terry "T-child"

Till then.
P.T.O

Remembers ARTISTS will meet be it in heaven cihisuls earth or hell.

# FORCIBLE LOVE

Nice play that portrays the problems and the life Style of African artist present, Struggling Future to be and the past. not forgetting the Late John Mwafangeyo may his Soul rest in peace

He gave as Art and we shall pray it in his Beloved NAME— WITHOUT FEAR OR FAVOUR....

Terence ART Lines.
Kaoma Zambia

14.

## KUNS EN VERMAAK  *Onder redaksie van Jo-Maré Duddy*

# Muafangejo-stuk tref wyd

FORCIBLE Love, die twee-
musiekdrama oor die lewe
van John Muafangejo wat
NTN tydens die onafhank-
likheidsviering gaan aan-
bied, het internasionale
belangstelling gewek.

Terence Zeeman, di-
rekteur van NTN en regis-
seur van dié stuk, het die
tagtigerwerk bewoning dat
die BBC 'n televisiespan
na Namibië gaan stuur om
'n dokumentêre program
oor die lewe van Muas-
fangejo staan te stel en dat
die span van materiaal uit
Forcible Love gebruik
gaan maak.

Zeeman het voorts be-
kend gemaak dat begin is
met reëlings om Forcible
Love by die wêreldbekende
Edinburg-kunsfees op te

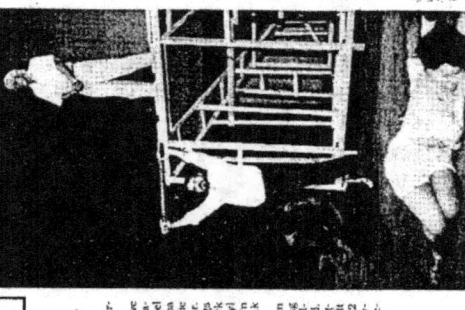

Allen Ambor

voer.

Forcible Love het
voortgevloei uit 'n unieke
spanpoging en werk-
winkel. Zeeman en Onde
Levinson was verantwoor-
delik vir die afkyk van die
teks. Vir dié doel het Levinson, wat oor 'n groot
Muafangejo-versameling,
die kopieregspiël kunste-
naar se werk en van sy
gereedskap beskik, voort-
durend tussen Oxford en
Windhoek beweeg.

Levinson is ook die ar-
tistieke direkteur van
Forcible Love.

Mees Xleen, hoof van
drama by NTN wat op die
punt staan om vir rege-
maande in Portugal te
gaan 'werk, vertolk drie
rolle in Forcible Love. Die

Suid-Afrikaanse akteur
Allen Ambor is spesiaal ingevoer om die rol van die
verteller te vertolk. Ambor

is bekend vir sy optredes
in die ou en nuwe Ruim-
teteater en die Baxter-
teater in Kaapstad en het
voorts jare vir Truk ge-
speel.

Banana Shekupe, wat
die rol van Muafangejo
vertolk, is nie net die stig-
terslid van Ndilmani nie,
maar is ook een van vyf
akteurs wat deel uitmaak
van die kulturele uitruilprogram tussen Namibië
en Denemarke.

Altesame 22 akteurs
tree in Forcible Love op.
Heelparty van die Ndis-
lmani-groep is eenvoudig in
Kotutura gewerf en aan
die skouspelagtige sang-
en danstonele in Kwan-
yama deel te neem. Hier is
dit veral 'n groep Kwan-

yama-kindertjies wat har-
te sal steel.

Hoewel Forcible Love
oor die lewe van Mua-
fangejo handel, is 'n veel
dieper en universele tema
onderliggend: die van die
wese van 'n kunstenaar.
Uit reptitsiebywonings
blyk dit dat die teks sterk
potensiaal het, terwyl
Forcible Love beslis 'n
visuele en klank-impak
het.

Forcible Love word van
Donderdag tot Saterdag
om 18h00 in die Wind-
hoek-Teater aangebied.
Toegang vir Donderdag-
aand is gratis, terwyl dit
R5 vir volwassenes en R2
vir studente vir die oorblywende twee vertonings be-
loop.

'n Toneel uit Forcible Love. Op die foto kan Daphné
de Klerk, Banana Shekupe, Terence Zeeman en
Mees Xleen gesien word.

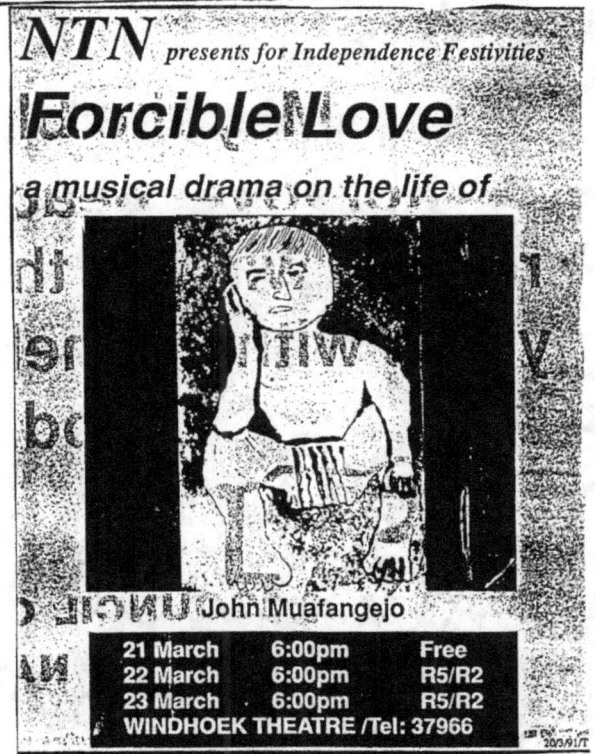

# Skouspel oor lewe van Muafangejo

ELEPHANT IS KILLING A LION IN A FUNNY WAY IN 1975.

'n Oorspronklike uitstalling van die werk van die grafiese kunstenaar John Muafangejo word tans in die voorportaal van die Windhoek-teater en die Kunsvereniging aangebied. Die uitstalling val saam met NTM se musiekdrama oor die lewe van Muafangejo, Forcible Love, wat van môre tot Saterdag in die Windhoek-teater opgevoer word.

FORCIBLE Love, die musiekdrama oor die lewe van John Muafangejo wat NTM tydens die onafhanklikheidsfeeste gaan aanbied, het internasionale belangstelling gewek.

Terence Zeeman, direkteur van NTM en regisseur van die stuk, het die afgelope week beweer dat die BBC 'n televisiespan na Namibië gaan stuur om 'n dokumentêre program oor die lewe van Muafangejo saam te stel en dat dit span van materiaal uit Forcible Love gebruik gaan maak. Zeeman het voorts bekend gemaak dat begin is met reëlings om Forcible Love by die wêreldbekende Edinburgkunstefees op te voer.

Forcible Love het voortgevloei uit 'n unieke samewerking en werksverhouding tussen Oxford en Windhoek beweg.

Levinson is ook die artistieke direkteur van Forcible Love.

drama by NTM wat op die punt staan om vir agt maande in Portugal te gaan werk, vertolk die rolle in Forcible Love. Die Suid-Afrikaanse akteur Allen Ambor is spesiaal ingevoer om die rol van die verteller te vertolk. Ambor is bekend vir sy optredes in die en en nuwe Ruimtenteater en die Baxterteater in Kaapstad en het voorts jare vir Truk gespeel.

Banana Shekupe, wat die rol van Muafangejo vertolk, is nie net die stigterlid van Nölltimani nie, maar is ook een van vyf akteurs wat deel uitmaak van die kulturele uitruilprogram tussen Namibië en Denemarke.

Alhoewel 22 akteurs tree in Forcible Love op. Hedparty van die geselskap is eenvoudig in

Katutura gesoek om aan die skouspelagtige sang- en danstonele in Kwanyama deel te neem. Hier is dit veral 'n groep Kwanyama-kindertjies wat hartie sal steel.

Hoewel Forcible Love oor die lewe van Muafangejo handel, is 'n studie dieper en onderliggend: dit van die wese van 'n kunstenaar. Uit repitisiebywonings

blyk dit dat die teks sterk potensiaal het, terwyl Forcible Love beslis 'n visuele en klank-inpak het.

Forcible Love word van Donderdag tot Saterdag om 18h00 in die Windhoek-T-eater aangebied. Toegang vir Donderdagaand is gratis, terwyl dit R5 vir volwassenes en D2 vir studente vir die oorblywende twee vertonings beloop.

WEDNESDAY MARCH 20 1991

# Forcible Love

Forcible Love is a musical drama based on the life of the Namibian graphic artist John Muafangejo, whose work makes an indelible impression on those coming into contact with it.

However, there was more to him than just his artistic talent.

His biography is a writer's dream and that is why Orde Levinson decided to base a stage production on the life of this humble man.

in three different roles directed by Terence Zeeman will give three performances tomorrow, Friday and Saturday at 18h00 in the Windhoek Theatre.

An interesting aspect of this production is that it features unemployed workers who were seen hanging around on the streets and after being auditioned, have proven to be singers and dancers of no mean talent.

The production is presented with an exhibition of Muafangejo's work at the NTN's acting company with Mees Xteen Arts Association.

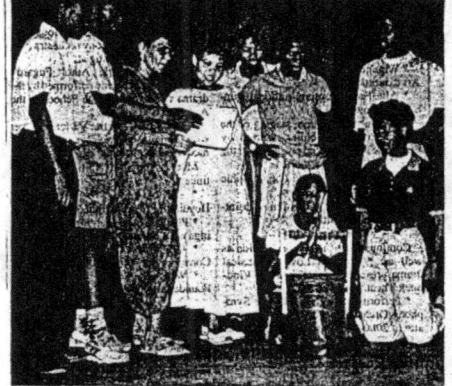

The NTN company who will give "life" to John Muafangejo on whose life the drama Forcible Love is based.

# "Forcible Love"?

Windhoek/al - Das National Theater von Namibia inszenierte zur Unabhängigkeitsfeier das von Orde Levinson geschriebene Stück "Forcible Love". Es handelt von der dramatischen Lebensgeschichte des über die Landesgrenzen hinaus bekannten namibischen Künstlers John Muafangejo.

Die Jugend im Ovamboland und die durch depressive Schübe gekennzeichnete Ausbildungszeit in Rorke's Drift sind ebenso szenisch verarbeitet, wie die Jahre künstlerischen Schaffens in Odipo und Windhoek und sein unerwarteter Tod durch Harzversagen in der Hauptrolle als John Muafangejo ist Bennan S... pe zu sehen sein. Mee Xteen spielt drei Rollen. Der Freier, der ein am ... aus Kapstadt engagierte Alan Ambor fungiert als Chronist

Für die Tanz- und Gesangseinlagen gelang es Shekupe und Xteen etliche talentierte Arbeitslose von den Straßen Windhoeks weg auf die Bühne zu engagieren. Sie veranschaulichen zum Beispiel Muafangejos künstlerische Arbeitsweise in der Form eines afrikanischen Tanzes

Die Regie für dieses erste lokale Musical führt der neue Theaterdirektor Terace Zea man. Gleichzeitig mit den Aufführungen am 21.-22. und 23. März kann im Foyer des Theaters eine Ausstellung der Linolschnitte John Muafangejos besichtigt werden.

Ort und Zeit: Windhoek Theater, am 21.-22. und 23. März, jeweils um 18 Uhr Eintritt am ersten Abend... nächst... gezeigt, sehen... nicht...

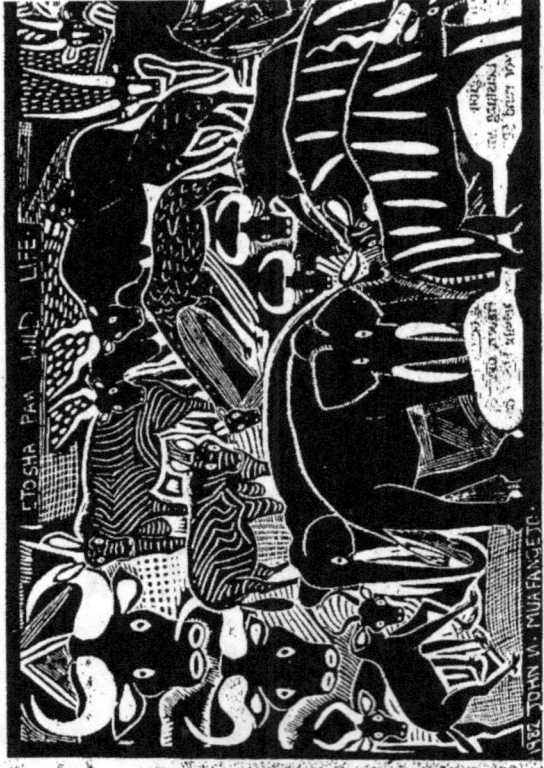

ETOSHA PAN WILD LIFE

BY JOHN W. MUAFANGETO

Den Originaltanz... "Etosha" Linolschnitt von John Muafangejo. In der Ausstellung in der Künstlern...

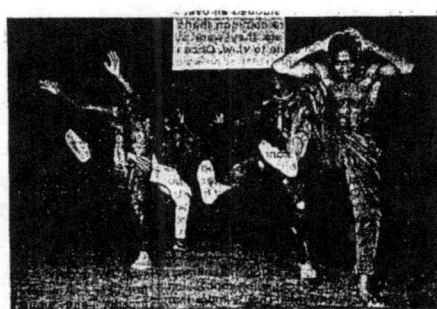

'Jobless but not useless, they are. These Kwanyama dancers who were taken from street corners where they hang around with other unemployed, will make their professional debut on stage this evening in the opening performance of the musical drama Forcible Love. Staged by NTN, this play based on the life of the late Namibian artist John Muafangejo will commence at 18h00 in the Windhoek Theatre. Principal actors are Banana Shekupe, Mees Xteen and Allen Ambor as the narrator. This evening's performance is free, being NTN's contribution towards the independence celebrations. The entrance fee for tomorrow and Friday, also at 18h00, will be R5 for adults and R2 for students and children.

# A force to be reckoned with

WHATEVER you think of its controversial subject matter, the NTN's "Forcible Love" puts the company fairly and squarely on the drama map and justifies its claim to the title 'national' theatre.

After a series of false starts, broken promises and unfulfilled potential dating way back, the NTN finally hit the mark with its Independence offering based on the life of artist John Muafangejo which opened on Thursday night to a packed house.

Under the directorship of Terence Zeeman, who took over at the theatre only last month, the company produced a show which bore all the signs of a confident, emergent national theatre ready to play a key role in Namibia's new cultural identity.

Workshopped from a script by Ordo Levinson, with a liberal dose of inspired direction from Zeeman, 'Forcible Love' broke new ground in several respects.

Its most daring move - prompted by lead actor Banana Shekupe - was to incorporate the dance work of 14 unemployed men, women and children with no previous theatre experience. Flying in the face of conservatives who saw the idea as an insult to professional theatre and liberals who condemned it as patronising, the gamble paid off well.

The work of the dancers, which sets the pace of the show with a dynamic Kwanyama wedding scene, was one of its highlights. The capacity audience was soon clapping and cheering as dancer after dancer dismissed any lingering impressions that theatrical talent has to be trained.

The main bulk of the show's action was taken care of by the NTN's core theatre with support from members of the Windhoek Players group. As John Muafangejo, Shekupe was by turns fiercely determined and fighteningly vulnerable. He trod the tightrope story of a man battling with insanity, with a confidence well beyond his comparatively short experience of professional theatre. In the scenes which showed Muafangejo in the grip of madness and in the moment of death, Shekupe was particularly convincing. A combination of good lighting, disciplined supporting mime, and concentration from the lead actor gave the death scene the sort of intensity which is often missing from a workshopped production's more poignant moments.

With the exception of the newspaper interview scene and a laborious discussion of the play's title towards the end of the show, "Forcible Love" created its own life-force. If the scenes were meant as a contrast, they didn't work. They were unnecessarily didactic and suggested a lack of confidence in the play's ability to do its job effectivley.

Even the use of the narrator - a helpful linking device given the play's diversity - bordered on overstatement at times. The final lines of the play in particular wrapped the whole story up far too neatly and didn't give the audience credit for being able to draw its own conclusions.

As with the dancers, the more innovative linking device of flashing giant slides of Muafangejo's work paid dividends. There were odd occasions when it distracted from the action, but mainly the projections served to underline themes and guide the audience rather than force it towards an idea. If the play dealt with generally sombre material, Zeeman used the slides to temper the intensity. As Muafangejo's classmates disturb his study with casual flirtation, the artwork above reads "The love is approaching but too much of anything is very dangerous".

Of his three separate roles, Mees Xteen was most impressive as Muafangejo's art teacher. The scene in which the class meets its impish new instructor is delightful. With Xteen's assured performance and cleverly assembled stage pictures, the audience is whipped through a lesson on art with never a twinge of being lectured to.

The same is true of Muafangejo's University of Cape Town interview when heavy monologue is nicely spread, with the artist slogging uphill through a panel of judges who desert him one by one leaving him finally alone.

Criticism has already been levelled that the play is too accusatory, misleading, too frivolous, downplays the role of the war, overplays that of the church. Undoubtedly the controversies surrounding Muafangejo's unhappy life will continue, but the show as a well-directed, well-acted professional piece of the theatre is easily capable of shouldering questions of interpretation.

With this production, the NTN cast looks more and more like a tight, professional troupe, while individual actors such as Norman Job and Daphne de Klerk command attention with increasing confidence. The production could do with some fine tuning - the dramatic 'scoop' of the first bishop scene, for example, is slightly mistimed - but the overwhelming impression created by "Forcible Love" is that the NTN has found its feet.

Already there have been invitations from Europe asking the company to tour, suggestions that it gets involved in theatre exchange schemes, and interest in filming from the BBC.

All these are exciting compliments but one hopes the company will remember that one swallow doesn't make a summer. The task of building a substantial national theatre which can feed into all areas and all communities of the country is a massive one. The NTN's work in Namibia is well and truly mapped out - and 'Forcible Love' proves the company is equal to it.

ONCE more from the top (of the theatre): members of the cast and production team of "Forcible Love" with the Muafangejo banners from Wembley. See story, page 5.

# From Wembley to Windhoek:
## Mufuangejo banners 'fly high'

REMEMBER the massive Mufuangejo backdrops used at the Mandela Is Free concert in Wembley attended by the newly-released ANC leader himself?

Well, one of them is now hanging outside the National Theatre of Namibia in Windhoek and the rest are on their way.

Just in time for the NTN production, the "handshake banner" was draped over the top of the theatre building this week by cast members of "Forcible Love", a drama based on the life of Namibian art legend John Mufuangejo.

According to director Terence Zeeman, the show is "ready to go". It opens on Thursday night for a free performance at the NTN's celebration of Namibia's first independent birthday. "It's turned out to be much bigger than we originally envisaged," said Zeeman, who has been working on the production since taking charge of the theatre at the beginning of last month. Some mention of his promise is that the drama has now been listed as part of the official Independence programme, and that the Swedish Ambassador in Namibia has expressed an interest in taking the production to Sweden.

With a combined cast of NTN players, Windhoek Players and 14 unemployed men and women who joined the theatre for the Mufuangejo production, "it's starting to look like a real

show", said Zeeman. "All we need now is the audience!"

Interest in the play's subject matter will probably guarantee a good turnout for its first-day run. Nevertheless the NTN office was buzzing with activity as invitations were issued, tickets printed and publicity pushed.

Everyone was excited as the Wembley banner was unfolded. Standing on the roof of the theatre with only three days to go and with the rest of the cast was on a definite "high".

Author of the "Mufuangejo" play, Oode Levinson, had brought the banner back with him from England last week. "It's turned out great — the rest will arrive by ship by the middle of the year.

"When the Wembley concert organisers first gave permission to use the Mufuangejo designs, it was on condition they sent out unused banners to Namibia", said Levinson.

"He said the massive interest in Mufuangejo was highlighted particularly in Britain where a tour of the artist's work was doing a six-week long round of the country's top museums. A BBC director would be present on the opening night of "Forcible Love" to see the performance and compile material for a one-hour pro-

gramme on Mufuangejo on British TV", said Levinson.

He said a number of comments written in the visitors book during the Mufuangejo tour had been included as items in the show. From fiercely critical ("Left-wing rubbish"), to analytical ("it just shows technique is not important") to admiring ("but just LOOK at the technique"), the comments revealed a fascination for the subject, as well as strong emotional involvement ("cry and pray for South Africa").

According to visiting Zambian theatre director Terence Mnyanda, who has been present for many rehearsals of "Forcible Love", the production is "one of the most exciting things I've seen". Due to leave Windhoek this week, he has postponed his return home for a week just to see the opening night.

A strong vote of confidence for anyone wondering whether a night at the theatre would be a good way to celebrate independence.

# FORCIBLE LOVE

Photos and stories by Kayele M. Kambombo

"Forcible love" is play based on the life a Namibian artist, late John Mwafangeyo. The play will be staged at the Windhoek Theatre on 21 - 23 March. The performers are all Namibians by birth.

The author of the play is Orde Levinson, the narrator is Allen Ambor and the director is Trence Zeeman. Banana Shekupe will act in the play as John Mwafangeyo.

It is a moving act and the entrance fee is R8. The evening will be free of charge.

The author, Levinson is born in Namibia and has written quite a number of plays, he has studied in South Africa and then at the Oxford University. Most of his plays have been performed in Cape Town at Space and in England.

Levinson got interested in the graphic work of Mwafangeyo and started collecting the artist work since 1973. Of recent, Levinson has also written a catalogue on Mwafangeyo's work which will be published next year.

He has organised for Mwafangeyo's graphics to be shown at the British museum. And the BBC will be here to do a documentary on Mwafangeyo's work.

"What interested me in his work and write this play is the fact that his (Mwafangeyo) life seemed to have examplify what a true artist

to. The title of the play came from his work", explained Levinson.

Asked to elaborate on the play itself, he said the play "is not just about Mwafangeyo, but it's about conflict, preasure and about forcible love". The actors have rehearsed for two weeks only "because of budget limitation". Thus the play was condenced from three acts to one. Another play that is in the pipe line will be the "Kwanyama marriage" (Efundula leengoma).

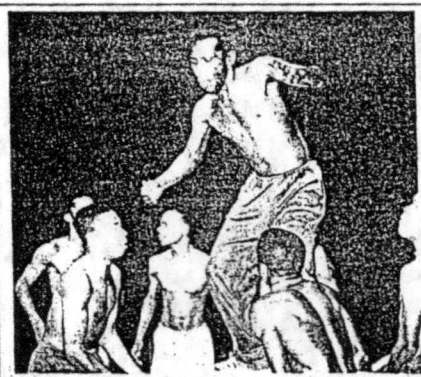

Banana Shekupe acting as John Mwafangeyo in the play (standing on top of thetable).

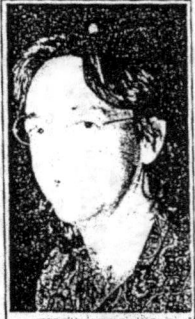

THE AUTHOR: Orde Levinson

Anything on culture? Phone Kayele M. Kambombo at Tel or Fax:229150

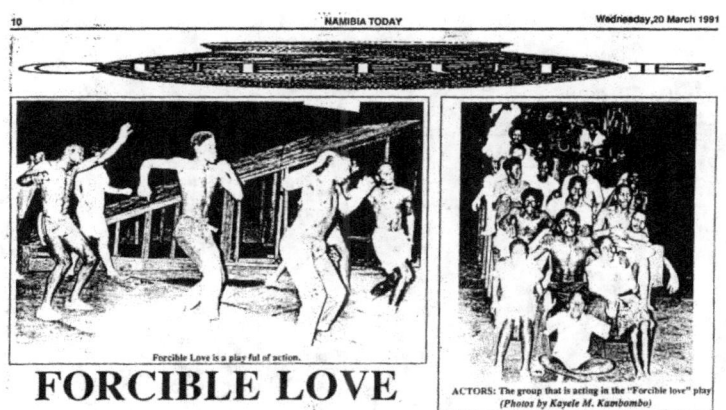

Forcible Love is a play ful of action.

ACTORS: The group that is acting in the "Forcible love" play
*(Photos by Kayele M. Kambombo)*

# FORCIBLE LOVE

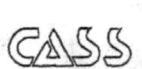

**CASS** Centre for Applied
Social Sciences

(Namibia Project)

Werner Hillebrecht
CASS Documentation Unit
P O Box 30822
Windhoek
Republic of Namibia
Tel: (+264)(61)229977
Fax: (+264)(61)225336

2 April 1991

Mr Orde Levinson
Magdalen College
Oxford University
Fax 0944-865-794846

By Fax
No. of pages: 3
In case of garbled or incomplete
transmission please call back

Dear Mr Levinson,

please find attached a bibliography of Muafangejo, as far
as literature was recorded in Namlit. Certainly there is
more literature, maybe in art journals, or in form of
exhibition brochures, which I was not able to consult.
I'd be thankful if you could help me to record more
material.

There is no charge on reasonable non-commercial
literature queries from Namlit.

It would be nice if you could inform me about the planned
publication. Im a preparing to launch a periodical
Namibian Research Newsletter, which will inform about new
and forthcoming publications, resources, and research
projects.

Let me conclude by congratulations for the Muafangejo
play, which my friends and myself greatly enjoyed, and
which marks the beginning a definitely new era in
Namibian theatre!

Yours

(Werner Hillebrecht)

# Note by the Publisher 2013

| | |
|---|---|
| Mæg ic be me sylfum | I can make a true song |
| soðgied wrecan, | about me myself, |

The Seafarer, date unknown.(Approximate translation of the old English)

Song, established in 2013  is an imprint of a new publication house, a division of Song of the Wild Swan Ltd.

It publishes any writings from anyone who has a song.

Song also participates in the BEL (Barter Exchange Levy) Price System.

## List of Selected Works by orde

Song, November 2013
*Areas of classification may overlap*

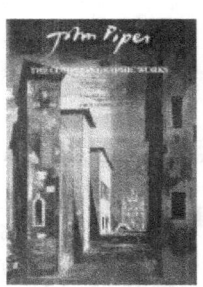

### Books

1.   *John Piper – The Complete Graphic Works: A Catalogue Raisonné 1923-1983*. Compiled and edited by Orde Levinson. Faber & Faber, 1988.

2.   *I Was Lonelyness: The Complete Graphic Works of John Muafangejo 1968-1987*. Struik Winchester, 1992. Foreword by Archbishop Desmond Tutu. Contributing essays from: Olga Levinson (The Life and Art of John Muafangejo); Edward Lucie-Smith (John Muafangejo); Pat Gilmour (On Not Being a Political Artist); Orde Levinson (John Muafangejo, Cubism and Traditional African Art); Olga Levinson (The Historical Development of Art in Namibia) and Steven Sack (The Rorke's Drift Art and Craft Centre) and all Muafangejo's Interviews, Statements and published conversations.

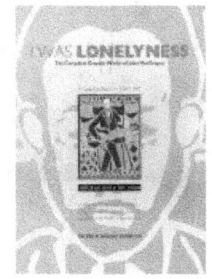

3.   *The African Dream – Visions of Love and Sorrow. The Art Of John Muafangejo*. Thames and Hudson, 1993. Foreword by Nelson Mandela.

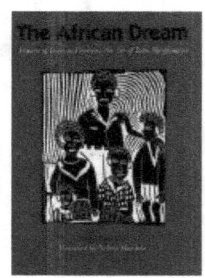

4.   *Quality and Experiment. The Prints of John Piper – A Catalogue Raisonné*. Lund Humphries, 1996.

5.   *The Prints of John Piper – A Catalogue Raisonné 1921-1991*. Lund Humphries, 2010. Contributing essays: Introduction (Orde Levinson); Experiment and Quality (Orde Levinson); Subject and Technique in Piper's Printmaking (David Fraser Jenkins); Working

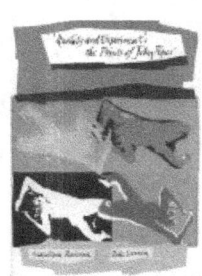

with Printers (John Piper).

6    *Hitting the Nail on the Head – The Complete Written Works of John Piper 1913-1992.* An estimated three volumes with contributing essays by various authors (tba). Scheduled for publication 2014/5.

7    *Delights and Aphorisms, selected writings of John Piper.* Scheduled for publication 2014-5.

8    *Daniel Henry Kahnweiler: A bibliography.* Scheduled for publication 2014.

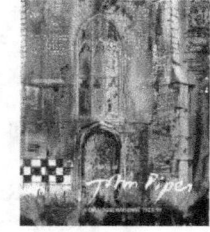

9    *The Life and Work of Daniel Henry Kahnweiler: A critical evaluation.* Originally part of the D. Phil. Study at Magdalen College, Oxford University. Scheduled for publication 2015.

10    *The Complete Writings of Daniel Henry Kahnweiler.* Three volumes. Scheduled for publication 2015-6.

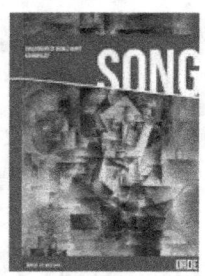

## Conversations and interviews

11    *orde's Conversations with Henry Moore.* Henry Moore talks about influences, the artists he likes, his work and life in general. Available as eBook 2013  Book published by Song 2014

12    *Orde's Conversations with Richard Sorabji (videoed)* in progress,. Richard Sorabji in thought and in person is brought to us in a unique experiment where orde has selected friends from each decade to converse with him. Completed to date are Louis Hynes (age 10); Laurence Hutton-Smith (age 20); Richard Kuziara (age 37); Lisa Hammond-Marty (age 40-50); Jeremy Rowe (age 50-58); Marianne Talbot (age 58--68)  Joanna Foster (age 68-80). Available as video, eBook and book. Scheduled publication 2015.

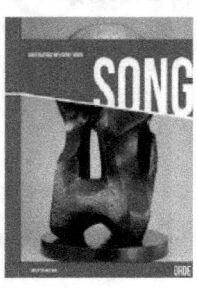

13    *Talking to Solly Irwin (videoed)*
Schedule publication as eBook and book 2014-5,

## Films

14     *Essences*. Independent production
produced by orde under the inspiration of
Straub and Huillet. A contemplative
mood piece starring Richard E. Grant
and Kiki Savejan
Director/script/editor: orde
Cast: Richard E Grant, Kiki Savejan
Running Time: 40 minutes/colour
Date Completed: 1983
(Image: Scene Shot from Essences by orde.)

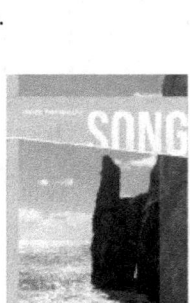

15     *Ÿ*
Director/script/editor: orde
Cast: Richard E Grant
Running time:16 minutes/colour
Date Completed: c.1987.

## Film scripts

16     *The Judgment of Shylock*. In progress.

## In fermentation/digestion

17     *The Inventors dilemma*. A novel?
18     *Five Fingers are not the same*. A novel?
19     *Turquoise*. A love story.
20     *The Weather of myself*. A philosophical book/diary.
21     *The Human Tragedy*. A true story, novel/poem?

## Music

22     *I am here thank you please, a musical
composition*. Contains an introduction on
classical and romantic by orde.
Available 2014 as eBook and book (published
by Song.

23     *Le Bordel Philosophique*. A musical composition
with 5 contemporary composers (George

Barton, Sam Fernando, Cheryl Francis-Hoad, Simon Roth, Jaime Wolfson). A composition based on a poem, which is based on a painting to reach a musical gesamtkunstwerk for our era. Scheduled for completion 2014.

## Plays

24     *Forcible Love.* A play based on the life of John Muafangejo.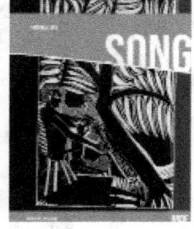

25     *Forcible Love (NTN version).* A musical on the life of John Muafangejo - premiered at the National Theatre, Windhoek, Namibia for the Independence Celebrations. Includes reviews. Available 2014 as eBook and book (published by Song)

26     *The Rialto Dialogues.* Described as a revolutionary work about the Merchant of Venice by William Shakespeare. It includes the entire work uncut but introduces 4 new characters to open a meaning and channel to one of Shakespeare's greatest plays. Available 2014 as eBook and book (published by Song)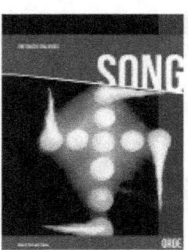

27     *Shylock the Magnificent.* A play 13 years after the Trial Scene of the Merchant of Venice by Shakespeare. Available 2014 as eBook and book (published by Song) See also The Soul's Heritage under poems.

## Poems

28     *Miscellaneous poems.* Short poems found over the years. Available 2014 as eBook and book.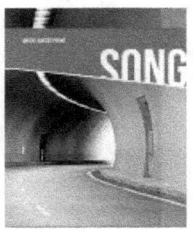

29     *The Love song of D. Adolph Hitler.* In progress.

30     *Der Tod Des Miguel.* In progress

31     *Les Dem.* About Picasso's painting *Les Demoiselles D'Avignon*, includes essay on *Les Dem* by Professor Andrew Laird. Available 2014 as eBook and book (published by Song).

32      *Ndilapa Nkosi.* A lyrical comedy, first part of *The Soul's Heritage,* a trilogy, a landmark work described by Samuel Beckett as a 'moving feat'. Includes reviews and responses from various persons including Beckett.
Available 2014 as eBook and book (published by Song).

33      *Antomat Diplony of the Orb.* An epic comedy, in progress, second part of The Soul's Heritage, a trilogy.

34      *The Argonauta Vineyard.* A tragic comedy, in progress, third part of The Soul's Heritage, a trilogy.

35      *Parlez à Voir.*
Available 2014 as eBook and book (published by Song).

36      *Flying strongly on one wing.*
Available 2014 as eBook and book (published by Song).

37      *Snowflakes and Ashes.*
Available 2014 as eBook and book (published by Song).

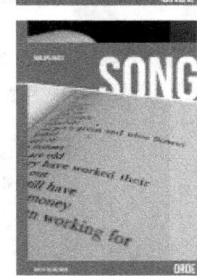

**Reviews and articles**

38      A number of articles and reviews exist and are being collated.

39      *Art, An Adaptive Function?*
Encyclopaedia of Evolution Mark Pagel (Editor-in-Chief), Oxford University Press, 2002. (365 articles from 330 different authors).

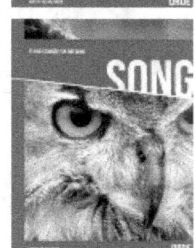

**Visual works**

      Drawings, paintings, photography, prints, sculptures
Please see www.orde.info

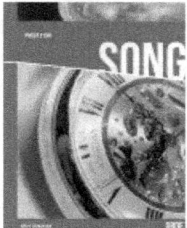